ADELPHI

PAPER · 290

CONTENTS

GLOSSARY

CFE	Conventional Armed Forces in Europe
CFSP	Common Foreign and Security Policy
CIS	Commonwealth of Independent States
CJTF	Combined Joint Task Forces
CSCE	Conference on Security and Cooperation in Europe
DG-Ia	Directorate-General for External Political Relations of the European Commission
EC	European Community
EFTA	European Free Trade Association
EMS	European Monetary System
EMU	Economic and Monetary Union
EP	European Parliament
EPC	European Political Cooperation
ERM	Exchange Rate Mechanism
EU	European Union
GATT	General Agreement on Tariffs and Trade
IAEA	International Atomic Energy Agency
IEPG	Independent European Programme Group
IGC	Intergovernmental Conference
NAC	North Atlantic Council
NACC	North Atlantic Cooperation Council
NATO	North Atlantic Treaty Organisation
NPT	Nuclear Non-Proliferation Treaty
PFP	Partnership for Peace
SACEUR	Supreme Allied Commander Europe
START	Strategic Arms Reduction Talks
UN	United Nations
UNPROFOR	United Nations Protection Force
UNSC	United Nations Security Council
WEU	Western European Union
WEUCOM	WEU Telecommunication System

The Strategic Implications of European Integration

INTRODUCTION

When the process of European Union (EU) began in 1990–91, it seemed realistic that Western Europe would become a major actor in international security, given the new strategic environment and the redistribution of political weight at the end of the Cold War. Some West Europeans had visions of a more integrated Europe – based on a single market, a common currency and common foreign, security and defence policies – assuming the status of a third, if not a super, power situated between the Soviet Union and the United States. Consequently, until the break-up of the Soviet empire, Washington had been deeply concerned that European integration could undermine the North Atlantic Treaty Organisation (NATO) and rival America's leadership in Western security policies.

Now, the picture has changed significantly. The Soviet Union no longer exists and new states have been created on its former territory, with Russia as the dominant regional power. In the US, the Clinton administration is bringing its external commitments more into line with domestic demands, thus reducing the costs and risks of engaging in European and worldwide security. This has already led the US to adopt a more positive attitude towards the concept of a European defence identity. In Europe, however, any euphoria engendered by the signing of the Maastricht Treaty on European Union in December 1991 has disappeared. Instead, scepticism, if not pessimism, over the future of European integration has spread in response to the deep economic recession, the European monetary crisis, the Yugoslav debacle and the problems encountered during the ratification of the Maastricht Treaty. Many West Europeans believe that economic and monetary union (EMU), an important corner-stone in the construction of Europe, is an illusion and that support for renationalising foreign and security policies is much stronger than that for a common European policy.

However, the reasons for such pessimism are as exaggerated as were those for euphoria. It is true that the Maastricht Treaty only entered into force, after much difficulty and delay, on 1 November 1993. The resultant European Union is weak and by no means federal, and hopes for developing a truly common foreign, security and eventually defence policy have been significantly dampened. But not everything has gone wrong in the last three years. There is now regular dialogue among the foreign ministers of EU states on all aspects of security and, with closer cooperation of the Western European Union (WEU), European integration aims to respond to major strategic challenges. By completing negotiations with four European Free Trade Association (EFTA) countries on their accession to the EU and by promising membership to countries in Central and Eastern Europe, Western Europe may well contribute to the founding of a new order. This paper analyses both the problems created by what has already been achieved, and what European integration can be expected to achieve in the future for international security and European stability.

Assessing the security role of European integration in an era so profoundly different from that of the Cold War raises a number of important questions. What capabilities and major limitations does European integration have to contribute to regional order and international security? How far does European integration and its emerging security and defence dimension weaken or strengthen the long-established transatlantic security partnership? What are the consequences of constructing a new Europe through expanded integration?

These questions are addressed in three main chapters which look at the strategic implications of European integration from the perspective of the Twelve, the transatlantic community, and the wider Europe. Chapter I identifies the major problems of security integration as demonstrated by the negotiations on political union. It pays particular attention to the driving forces behind the Maastricht process and those factors which hampered the transfer of competence to Brussels. This chapter also analyses the strengths and weaknesses of the Union Treaty and assesses Western Europe's qualities as an international actor.

Chapter II focuses on events post-Maastricht and their consequences for the development of a common security and defence policy, and for the transatlantic security relationship. First, it analyses the impact of the Treaty's ratification problems, the implications of an EFTA enlargement, the problems of defining the content of a Common Foreign and Security Policy (CFSP) and the build-up of WEU. Second, and despite indications of a shift away from deeper union, it identifies those policy areas in which the CFSP and WEU can contribute to regional and international security. Third, it discusses the frictions present in transatlantic relations since the end of the Cold War and the beginning of the Maastricht process. Competition and cooperation between WEU and NATO, as well as the danger of a growing rift between both sides of the Atlantic, are a major focus of this chapter. Although the January 1994 NATO summit suggests that US–European tensions have been much reduced, a new, broader transatlantic partnership is required.

Chapter III deals with major challenges to peace and stability in the European system and evaluates the responses of the European Community(EC)/EU and its member-states. It analyses the limitations of a common security policy as demonstrated by Western Europe's management of the Yugoslav crisis and its impact on the EU's relations with its major

4

partners. The gargantuan task of integrating Central and Eastern Europe, thereby expanding the West European peace zone, is the second focus of this chapter which looks specifically at the different roles of NATO, WEU and the EC/EU. West Europeans cannot expect only other European states, notably in the East, to make changes. Western Europe itself has to change its attitudes and adapt its integration policies to the new requirements of post-Cold War Europe if it is to contribute to greater stability in Europe through both deepening and widening.

This paper does not cover all aspects of future integration. It discusses economic issues only where relevant to political unification. Nor does it analyse in detail attempts to develop a more coherent West European policy towards the Mediterranean, the Maghreb or the near East. This is largely because Western Europe needs to make substantial progress towards a CFSP before it can exert greater influence in other regions of strategic importance. The paper also leaves out certain risk factors such as uncontrolled mass-migration, drug trafficking or terrorism. Although not negligible factors in West European security, they can be better dealt with through a common immigration policy and closer cooperation among interior ministries rather than by security policies involving both foreign and defence ministries.

Assessing the strategic dimension of European integration is no easy task. The ability to contribute to humanitarian missions and peacekeeping in Europe and the wider world is certainly one indicator, particularly given the shift in focus from defence to crisis management. The ability to deal with economic and political sources of instability is another. Because the situation in Western Europe, and on the international scene, is in a continual state of flux, it is extremely difficult to draw a complete picture of the actual and potential implications of integration. It is not yet clear what future role the United States will play in European security and to what extent NATO may be transformed. While developments in Russia and other parts of the former Soviet Union remain unpredictable, their actual and potential risks are still an important part of NATO's *raison d'être*. The fledgling democracies in Central and Eastern Europe are facing serious economic and political problems and when and whether they can reach a phase of consolidation is still unclear. Moreover, nationalism is not confined to the eastern half of the continent, and a variety of centrifugal forces is making closer integration in Western Europe increasingly complex.

European integration is moving forward incrementally, without any grand strategy, according to the different security interests and political priorities of EU states. This paper focuses on the largely neglected longer-term implications of short-term policies for both the transatlantic relationship and European security. This includes the fundamental issue of whether Central and Eastern Europe can be integrated successfully without weakening the efficiency of existing institutions.

I. THE TWELVE AND MAASTRICHT

Since the early 1950s and the failure of the European Defence Community, several fruitless attempts have been made at both political and security integration among the EC countries.[1] In 1972 at its meeting in Paris, the European Council claimed that European Union could be achieved by 1980. In practice, however, the member-states preferred market integration to political and security integration, keen to preserve their national freedom of manoeuvre in the political sphere as far as possible. Thus, since 1970, European Political Cooperation (EPC) has developed on a purely intergovernmental level outside the confines of the Rome Treaty.[2] The agreement to discuss 'political and economic aspects' of security in the framework of the EPC received its contractual basis in Title III of the 1987 Single European Act. However, problems within the EPC/EC in reaching a consensus on creating a defence identity had already led in 1984 to the reactivation of WEU.[3] The aim was to use WEU as a forum for consultation and policy coordination between the foreign and defence ministers of its member-states. Yet, WEU remained in the shadow of NATO, and most WEU members showed only occasional interest in their institution.[4] Although Western Europe had some influence on East–West relations through the developing EPC, this was only the diplomatic side of security, and throughout the Cold War NATO and the US, as guarantors of Western Europe's security, had the effect of strictly limiting integration.

The idea of creating a European Union with a CFSP was relaunched following internal developments in the EC in the second half of the 1980s and the significant changes in the international environment post-1989. With the collapse of the Soviet empire, the direct threat to the security of Western Europe disappeared and West Europeans felt more secure and less dependent on the United States. This led to an attempt to deal with security- and defence-policy integration under new preconditions, and ideas which had first been aired in the 1950s (Europe as a third power) reappeared on the agenda. Internally, it was the 1987 Single European Act and the 1992 internal market programme which together created a new dynamic for the EC.[5] In June 1988, the European Council decided to link monetary integration to the completion of the single market and, 18 months later, it was agreed that monetary union would be negotiated in the framework of an Intergovernmental Conference (IGC). EC bodies began to discuss whether steps towards political integration should follow suit in order to reduce the growing gap between economics and politics. But the decisive impetus for political community-building came from German unification in 1989–90 which altered the internal power balance of the EC. Many EC states became increasingly willing to deepen integration in order to embed the new Germany in tight structures. Following the initiative of President

Mitterrand and Chancellor Kohl for political union in April 1990 and the ensuing decision of the Twelve in June 1990 to convene a second IGC in parallel to the one on monetary union, the Maastricht process was set in motion.[6]

Today, the interests of member-states vary according to domestic and international developments. In Germany scepticism is growing about the possibility and usefulness of constructing a federal Europe, in France on the liability of the West European option and in Britain on NATO's uncontested primacy in European security. Yet many of the basic interests which determined the security stipulations of the Maastricht Treaty are still relevant. Now that the Maastricht Treaty is in force, the EU's future contributions to European and international security must be defined. This can only be done on the basis of the Treaty's provisions which represent compromises in legal terms to keep the options of implementing both national policies and a more common foreign and security policy open.

Negotiating a CFSP
The IGC on political union (December 1990–December 1991) covered almost all policy areas. On the agenda was the introduction of European citizenship, social policies, consumer protection, development and immigration policies. The range of proposals for establishing a CFSP, unthinkable a few years earlier, was surprisingly broad, including suggestions for developing a Community arms-procurement policy; to introduce a mutual assistance clause; to make WEU subordinate to the European Council; and to apply majority voting to the CFSP.[7]

The practical approach to a CFSP was, however, much more gradual. The interests of the member-states differed markedly, and the lowest common denominator had to be found to ensure that all member-countries would ratify the Treaty provisions. The Americans (see Chapter II), although not present at the negotiations, expressed their views and concern to most EC governments, particularly during the first round of talks on political union.[8] While the IGC on political union was in progress, NATO was busy with its strategic review and many EC governments seemed to be waiting for NATO to announce its new concept before finalising their position on European defence.

THE FIRST ROUND (DECEMBER 1990–JUNE 1991)
The main players in the negotiations on political union were France, Britain and Germany. France and Britain were at loggerheads from the outset. Germany, while close to the French position, tried to balance its interests towards both Washington and Paris.

Roughly speaking, two groups negotiated the CFSP. The smaller group favoured British thinking and scepticism, while the larger group was closer to the Franco-German tandem. Britain adopted a rather restrictive stance towards European defence in order to prevent any undermining of NATO, preferring pragmatic reform of the EPC based on the principle of consensus.[9] While open to greater political cooperation between the EC member-countries, including all aspects of security policy, Britain believed that defence should remain with NATO and that the security policies of the Twelve should be closely coordinated with the Alliance. After the 1991 Gulf War, Britain wanted to strengthen WEU to prepare Western Europe better for out-of-area crises, but without subordinating WEU to the EU or the European Council. Instead WEU should serve as a bridge between NATO and the EU and strengthen the European pillar of the Alliance, particularly given the large-scale reductions in American troops stationed in Europe and concern that the lack of a European initiative for Western defence could further weaken the transatlantic security system.

The Netherlands and Portugal both supported the British position. The Lubbers government was even keener to accentuate the primacy of NATO, but in contrast to the British, the Dutch favoured a more federal type of Union. Portugal, with its traditional Atlantic orientation, also favoured a cautious approach to European defence. It was particularly reticent on the question of majority voting, fearing that a small country's sovereign voice could become marginalised or overruled by the larger ones. Denmark and neutral Ireland were also among the more reluctant countries, although for different reasons. Whereas Ireland insisted on a special clause to secure its status of neutrality, Denmark wanted to preserve NATO's role while also deepening European integration with a view to the need better to include the unified Germany.[10]

The second group of countries was in favour of establishing a CFSP with the perspective of a common defence to be written into the treaty on the future Union. France and Germany were its leading promoters, although neither could produce a concrete design for a CFSP. The Mitterrand–Kohl initiatives in April and December 1990 only outlined general ideas for the future Union, and while the first proposal in the framework of the IGC on political union was put forward in February 1991, a more detailed one did not materialise until October 1991.[11] Belgium, Luxembourg, Italy, Greece and, above all, Spain backed the Franco-German position.[12] Greece's approach was similar to that of the EC Commission in arguing for a mutual assistance clause and security guarantees.[13] But its bargaining power was marginal and its interests in security solidarity clearly had much to do with its dispute with Turkey. Italy was also in favour of a qualitative leap in community-building and even proposed merging WEU and the EC/Union.[14] But, in the course of negotiations, it modified its position and played the role of mediator between the 'continental' and the 'Atlantic' groups.

French interests in the security and defence dimension of European integration had only developed since 1989–90,[15] following the fundamental changes in the strategic environment, in particular German unification.[16] France wanted European security to be a mainly 'European' affair, implying a reduced role for NATO and the US, and for the new Germany to be 'controlled' by deeper integration. France's experience in the Gulf War also led it to conclude that US–British patronage was not acceptable, and it became more willing to entertain integration politics than ever before in the history of the Fifth Republic. In order to bridge the contradiction between Gaullist principles and European integration, Paris wanted the CFSP to be strictly separated from Community procedures with the European Council playing a leading role, and based on principles of intergovernmental cooperation (the only point on which it agreed with Britain). As long as the Union lacked a direct defence dimension, WEU should be closely linked to its decisions and politics.

The German government's interest in an EU went far beyond assuring its neighbours, notably France, that Germany would remain firmly anchored in Western structures (including NATO).[17] The Kohl government maintained Germany's traditional foreign-policy stance of uniting Europe through gradual integration in all relevant policy fields, including defence in the last stage. Although the German vision of a federal Europe conflicted with French views, Bonn accepted the guiding role of the European Council and, finally, also the intergovernmental nature of the CFSP.[18] The strengthening of Franco-German relations was the German *leitmotif* in the Maastricht process. In order to retain some of its communitarian approach, Bonn insisted on a greater role for the Commission in the CFSP and the introduction of possibilities for majority voting. It saw upgrading WEU as a temporary solution as long as full defence integration was impossible. But Bonn perceived the close relationship between WEU and the EU as a means of influencing the domestic climate regarding legitimising defence after the Cold War and the debate on participating in out-of-area operations. Thus the German government was strongly in favour of the perspective of a common defence, even if a federal Union was not in sight, and even if it conflicted with Germany's own interests in preserving NATO and maintaining strong ties with Washington. The conviction that developing a fully fledged Union would be a very long-term process assured Bonn of compatibility between Europe and NATO for the foreseeable future.

These basic interests influenced the debate until the Maastricht summit in December 1991 (and far beyond). The Luxembourg summit meeting of the European Council in June 1991 was unable to agree on the main points of a CFSP, above all because of the structure of the draft treaty drawn up by the Luxembourg presidency.[19] The CFSP, as well as justice and home affairs, was separated from the supranational structures of the EC. Generally speaking, Italy, Germany and others were still interested in a more integrated type of EU, and the Luxembourg summit seemed only to mark a

9

half-way station in the negotiations on political union. Moreover, the Twelve became involved in the escalating Yugoslav crisis, leading to different assessments of the possibilities and limitations of a CFSP.

THE SECOND ROUND (JULY–DECEMBER 1991)

The Dutch presidency produced a new draft treaty which was more integrated in nature.[20] Yet in this draft the EC – and not the EU – was to define and implement a CFSP, complementing the role of WEU and NATO. This was neither acceptable to France and Germany (because it devalued the role of the European Council) nor to Britain because it brought foreign and security policy under the auspices of the EC. Due to the lack of significant support for the Dutch draft treaty among member-states, negotiations then returned to the basic ideas of the Luxembourg draft treaty.

Some progress towards a mainstream consensus was made in October through an Anglo-Italian initiative and subsequent Franco-German proposals. On 4 October 1991, the British and Italian governments presented a joint 'Declaration on European Security and Defence' which proposed to found a Union that would gradually develop a CFSP in 'the longer term perspective of a common defence policy' to be 'compatible' with that of the Alliance. WEU would form the 'defence component' of the Union while at the same time strengthening 'the European pillar of the Alliance'. In this dual role WEU would 'take account' of European Council decisions without being subordinated to the EU. The proposal included creating a WEU Rapid Reaction Force for out-of-area crises, and establishing a military planning cell. In addition, it was suggested that WEU's headquarters should be transferred from London to Brussels and that links of association should be created between WEU and other 'European partners and allies'. Its role should be reviewed by 1998 when the parties of the modified Brussels Treaty would be free to relinquish their membership.

Shortly after the Anglo-Italian declaration, more detailed Franco-German proposals were sent to the Dutch EC presidency on 11 October (made public on 14 October).[21] In contrast to the Anglo-Italian initiative, Paris and Bonn stressed that the CFSP should ultimately include a common defence and that in the meantime the 'decisions and measures taken by the Union' in the area of security and defence should be 'developed and implemented entirely or in part' by WEU, which was defined as an 'integral part' of the EU development. The creation of 'an organic link' between WEU and the EU was proposed whereby WEU would 'act in conformity with the directives of the Union' and cooperate with NATO. The paper also included: a list of topics and policy areas for the future CFSP; proposals for the operative development of WEU including its transfer to Brussels; the creation of a planning cell (similar to the Anglo-Italian declaration); and specific suggestions for WEU's enlargement. The treaty provisions should be reviewed in 1996.

10

The paper briefly announced the strengthening of Franco-German military cooperation as well as the creation of a 'European corps' which could include forces of other WEU member-states. This phrase, which caused some friction among the other partners, underlined the willingness of France and Germany to go ahead in the defence fields. The idea of a Eurocorps also served some very concrete bilateral interests. One German aim was to leave open the option for maintaining French troops in Germany in response to the earlier announcement by President Mitterrand that French troops would be withdrawn from the territory of its neighbour following its regained sovereignty.

The last weeks before the Maastricht summit were marked by intense consultations at various levels. Whereas Britain stressed that WEU needed to be situated between the Union and NATO, France stressed the different nature of WEU's relations with NATO and with the Union. Consequently, France was against a double-hatting formula which would enable NATO forces, after consultation within the organisation, to be assigned to WEU tasks.[22] France neither wanted to be reintegrated into NATO through the back door, nor to grant the US a right of control over European military activities. Instead, Paris wanted more independent European defence arrangements only loosely tied to the US. Bonn, not wishing to alienate the Americans completely, declared that the forces it assigned to the Eurocorps would remain in NATO, but also agreed with Paris that only EU members could join WEU.

At the NATO summit in Rome on 7–8 November 1991, the 16 Western leaders agreed on diplomatic formulas covering the different interests of Alliance members including the US. Although the communiqué language used was open to interpretation, NATO's essential role (not its primacy) was agreed on and the importance of a European defence identity compatible with that of the Alliance was underlined.[23] The summit somewhat eased tensions between the British and French. But, despite several meetings of officials and foreign ministers, it proved impossible to agree on four points: majority voting in the area of the CFSP; the definition of a European defence identity; concrete relations between WEU and the EU as well as NATO; and whether a review in 1996 or 1998 should be general or committed to a specific task, such as merging WEU and the EU. These issues were left to be agreed by the heads of state and government at the Maastricht summit.

The Treaty on European Union
The Treaty on European Union,[24] as agreed by the 12 heads of state and government in Maastricht on 9–10 December 1991, is a document of compromise, but one which represents an important landmark in the process of European integration.[25] The two IGCs which led to the Treaty are

comparable only with the Conference of Messina which founded the European Economic Community in 1956–57.

The Treaty underlines the evolutionary character of an 'ever closer union' (the term 'federal' was avoided because of British resistance) based on three pillars: the amended EEC Treaty establishing a European Community and including monetary union (with a central bank and a common currency in its final stage); provisions for a CFSP; and the cooperation of member-states in domestic, judicial and police affairs. Annexed to the Treaty are various protocols and declarations, including two by WEU members. The declarations are not legally binding, but express the political will of governments.

The Maastricht Treaty does not lay the foundation for a United States of Europe, notwithstanding the introduction of European citizenship. It increases the complexity of policy-making in order to protect national sovereignty as far as possible. Overall, this strengthens the trends in European integration which were already discernible before the Maastricht process started:[26]

– the extension of the scope of common policies resulting from the magnetic pull of the EC, accompanied by the transfer of competencies to common institutions;

– the fact that the same institutions have to play a dual role in both Community affairs and intergovernmental cooperation. This can be interpreted either as 'communitarisation', or as undermining supranational structures;

– the growth in exception rules for certain member-states, thus leading to a more multi-layered structure or phased or multiple-speed integration. Examples include Britain's opting-out of the social chapter, the special rules for Britain and Denmark regarding monetary union, and the general stipulation that the final stage of monetary integration can begin even if not all member-states do meet the necessary economic preconditions to participate.

Stipulations for the CFSP

Title V, Article J, of the Treaty on European Union replaced the EPC as laid down in Title III of the Single European Act. The 12 governments also enlarged the scope of what was currently covered by the EPC to 'all' aspects of security policy, and attempted to introduce more binding rules. The word 'common' only expresses the intention to achieve greater unity in foreign and security policy, not that the CFSP will work in a communitarian way as, for example, does the common trade policy of the EC.

CFSP objectives are, *inter alia*: 'to safeguard the common values, fundamental interests and independence of the Union; to strengthen the security of the Union and its Member States in all ways; to preserve peace and strengthen international security' (J 1.2). These far-reaching objectives will be met through less ambitious means such as 'systematic cooperation' and the gradual implementation of 'joint action', but only in those areas 'in which the Member States have important interests in common' (J 1.3). Member-states who do not act in accordance with CFSP decisions cannot be sanctioned despite having committed themselves to support the Union's CFSP 'in the spirit of loyalty and mutual solidarity' (J 1.4). The Council has to check that 'these principles are complied with', while member-states ensure that their national policies conform with the CFSP. Yet, on the basis of these provisions, the psychological pressure on countries which do not follow the herd could be much greater than under the less committing rules of the previous EPC.

The contractual parties also expressed their willingness to uphold 'common positions' in international organisations and conferences, including those in which not all member-states participate (J 2.3). This applies to organisations such as the Conference on Security and Cooperation in Europe (CSCE), NATO (via WEU) or the United Nations (UN) and underlines the Union's intention to speak with one voice in these fora. Members of these and other international organisations are committed to an exchange of information among all the Twelve. In the case of the UN Security Council (UNSC), a compromise had to be reached between the British and French concern not to be restricted by CFSP mechanisms, and the intentions of other countries, such as Germany and Italy, to compensate for their non-membership in the UNSC. The Union Treaty thus states that the two West European permanent members of the UNSC have to 'ensure the defence of the positions and the interests of the Union' within that framework (J 5.4). How that will work in practice remains to be seen. The management of the Yugoslav crisis (see Chapter III) is not a good precedent and the policy option offered by the Union Treaty did not prevent Germany from seeking membership in the UNSC.

The most important part of Title V is Article J 4 which states that the CFSP deals with 'all questions related to the security of the Union, including the eventual framing of a common defence policy, which might in time lead to a common defence' (J 4.1). This wording is a compromise between mainly Franco-German intentions and British resistance. It proposes a common defence policy and perhaps a common defence, but without mentioning when and how. The answers to these major questions have been postponed until the revision of Article J 4 in 1996. Until then, WEU has to play a very specific role in European integration. The Treaty states that the Union can request 'WEU, which is an integral part of the development of the Union, to elaborate and implement decisions and actions of the Union which have defence implications' (Article J 4.2). Thus WEU remains a separate institution with a close working relationship with the Union which does not itself deal with defence. The Treaty also protects the 'specific character of the security and defence policy of certain Member States', a tribute to Ireland's neutrality. But other member-states also insisted that their special interests be preserved when the Treaty concedes that the Union's policy should be 'compatible' with that of NATO, should 'respect' obligations under the Washington Treaty and not 'prevent' closer cooperation within NATO, WEU and on a bilateral level (J 4.4 and 4.5).

The role of WEU in the European–US security architecture is outlined in two declarations annexed to the Treaty. In the first declaration, WEU is defined as 'the defence component of the European Union' and as the instrument 'to strengthen the European pillar' of NATO. To translate this double function into practice, the Nine agreed to develop WEU's operational role by defining 'appropriate missions, structures and means' and by establishing working relations with the EU (including synchronising Council and working group meetings), as well as with NATO, based on the principles of 'transparency' and 'complementarity'. The second declaration on enlarging WEU offered membership or observer status to EU members and associate status to other European NATO countries (see Chapter II).

It is difficult to assess whether British reserve or French intentions succeeded in Maastricht. It is true that defence has not yet become part of the EU and that WEU has links not only with the Union, but also with NATO. On the other hand, it is clear that the relationship between WEU and the EU is a special one and that, ideally, membership of both organisations should coincide.

CFSP DECISION-MAKING
The mechanisms for EU foreign and security policy-making include the European Council (made up of the heads of state and government), the Council of Foreign Ministers (previously only an EC body), the EC Commission and, in contractual external affairs, the European Parliament (EP).

The European Council is the central supervising body for both EC affairs and intergovernmental cooperation and it sets up the guidelines for the CFSP (J 8.1). The Council of Ministers defines and implements the CFSP (J 8.2). The dual structure of different EC bodies and EPC machinery, however, has been maintained to some extent which may still lead to inefficiency. Whereas the Committee of Permanent Representatives to the EC prepares all aspects of Council meetings, the Political Committee of the previous EPC, made up of political directors of the foreign ministries, will be responsible for elaborating the CFSP and monitoring its implementation (J 8.5).

The European Commission, together with the Council, ensures coherence between the CFSP and the external relations of the EC and contributes to the Union's representation in third countries through its virtually worldwide delegations (J 6). It now has the right to make proposals concerning the CFSP in the same way as member-states (J 8.3). This endows the Commission, which acts and thinks from a supranational viewpoint, with

14

some influence over the EU's foreign and security policy, even if it does not have a voting right.[27]

The EP, however, was not granted the role it wanted in the foreign and security policy field.[28] The Maastricht Treaty only mentions a consultation and information procedure. The EP has the right to 'ask questions', to make 'recommendations' and to hold an 'annual debate'. Nevertheless, the new EC Article 228 increases the EP's influence on the EU's relations with third countries. All major agreements with budgetary and legal implications (trade agreements, association and cooperation agreements, acceptance of new members) will need the EP's assent, a step towards democratising the Union's competencies in external affairs. However, it will also increase the complexity of internal decision-making because the EP may use its rights as an instrument in the institutional battle to strengthen its role.[29]

Another innovation is the introduction of majority voting in the area of foreign and security policy, although heavily restricted to procedural questions and only applicable in cases of joint action. Joint actions can be developed in areas of common interests (see Chapter II). At any stage of a joint action, the Council selects those matters where qualified majority voting can be applied by requiring 'at least 54 votes in favour, cast by at least eight members' (J 3.2). Member-states are generally committed to comply with agreed joint actions. But, as in so many areas of the Maastricht Treaty, there is an escape clause if a member-state has difficulties 'in implementing a joint action' (J 3.7).

There are doubts as to the practicability and efficiency of these regulations. Bearing in mind past experiences in Community policies, the new decision-making rules are expected to be used restrictively. On the other hand, many decisions cannot be made by majority voting while there is no federal European state with completely integrated foreign-policy and defence structures. This is particularly true in matters of war and peace when it is unacceptable for a member-state to risk the lives of its soldiers or citizens because it was over-ruled by a majority vote.

In general, consensus rule is the principal form of decision-making, thus perpetuating many of the Twelve's problems in responding efficiently to international crises. It is doubtful that any significant impetus will result from the restricted possibility to apply majority voting. It may also not help much that member-states expressed their political will to soften the consensus principle in foreign and security policy-making, declaring in one of the annexes to the Treaty on European Union their wish to 'avoid preventing a unanimous decision where a qualified majority exists in favour of that decision'.[30]

Conclusions

On the whole, the Maastricht Treaty reflects the most that could be achieved by the member-states after 34 years of European integration.

Although the Treaty was negotiated very carefully to preserve and improve the framework of the Treaty of Rome, many of its contractual provisions remain vague and open to interpretation according to the different interests of member-countries. This is particularly true for the CFSP, which raises doubts alone from a legal point of view about the possibilities of creating a truly common foreign and security policy. Moreover, while the stipulations for common defence express intentions and objectives, basic decisions on their realisation have been postponed until the next round of intergovernmental negotiations in 1996. Whether a qualitative jump to a more integrated foreign, security and defence policy can then be made is a very open question. The negotiations on the Union Treaty demonstrated the problem of political integration among sovereign nation-states, even with the common incentive of creating tighter political structures to control the unified Germany. But the German factor was only strong enough to work as a confederator not a federator because of the considerable unwillingness on the part of major actors (notably Britain, but also France) to accept limits being imposed on their political autonomy in a way that Germany would have been prepared to do. Similarly, visions of Europe as a strong power will remain blurred until member-states grant the Union the necessary means and responsibilities to assume such a role.

Be that as it may, integration *à la* Maastricht provides the framework for a more coherent West European policy through synthesising the EC, the CFSP and WEU, which may overcome some of the weaknesses of the previous EPC system. Even if the political aspects of the Maastricht Treaty fall far behind its economic ones, thus marking the fundamental imbalance between these two areas of integration, it sets out, for the first time, a contractual basis for political unification which orients the whole process of European integration.

In the short and mid-term, much of the Treaty's implementation will depend on the good will of its member-governments. To be pessimistic, the vagueness of many of the Treaty provisions could prevent the EU from becoming an efficient actor in international affairs, particularly when the interests of member-countries do not coincide.To be optimistic, the EU is evolutionary in character and the closer ties between the CFSP and the EC link the Twelve's foreign and security policy with the traditionally more dynamic aspects of EC integration.[31] Unfortunately, economic and monetary integration are themselves in deep crisis, thus dampening the hopes invested in a powerful logic of functionalism. These hopes were based on the notion that establishing economic and monetary union with the introduction of a common currency in the third stage, at the end of the 1990s, will inevitably strengthen Western Europe as an economic entity, which might in turn spill over to strengthen political and security integration. The third stage of monetary union can still proceed in 1999 because the European Monetary System (EMS) has been formally maintained, despite the crisis of its Exchange Rate Mechanism (ERM). But whether a common currency can be introduced depends on uncertain market developments and the necessary degree of economic convergence among the majority of member-states.

Regardless of whether any kind of plain functionalism will work between totally different policy areas, notably if favourable conditions do not exist for deeper economic integration, the EU is a rather complete international actor, not in terms of full competencies, but in terms of the scope of the policy areas covered by the new treaty. Diplomatic, economic and to some extent even military means (through WEU) allow the EU in principle to influence both European and world affairs. But the variety of procedures and institutions involved will not facilitate a consistent foreign and security policy. This is also true for the transatlantic dimension. NATO's security monopoly has definitely ceased to exist.[32] With the Maastricht Treaty now in force, Western security policies have to be coordinated by three bodies: NATO, WEU and the EU. Whereas there is no doubt that WEU has a double function *vis-à-vis* the Union and NATO, the direct relations between the Union and NATO remain largely undefined. As long as the EU's security policy remains compatible with that of the Alliance this should pose no serious problem. For some time to come the EU will also remain dependent for its security on NATO. Only NATO, with its direct links to US military capabilities, has sufficient means at its disposal to guarantee the security of all EU members (Ireland is a negligible case from a strategic point of view). This constellation, which will be put to the test by the EU's enlargement policies, could only change fundamentally if the US were to reduce its guarantees significantly and if West European defence structures were built up in such a way as to take over the core functions of NATO. An integrated European defence with a nuclear component would have radical implications for NATO and the transatlantic relationship. NATO would either have to become a bilateral alliance, or a completely new security arrangement would have to be set up between Europe and the US. Yet, these are speculations about options in a far distant future. In the nearer term, as the next chapter will show, interim steps had to be taken to resolve far more acute issues in both integration policies and transatlantic relations.

II. POST-MAASTRICHT DEVELOPMENTS AND THE COHESION OF THE WEST

After Maastricht, the rapid changes in the international environment caused by the break-up of the Soviet Union, the continuing war in Yugoslavia, and the emerging instabilities in Central and Eastern Europe created a markedly different situation from the pre-Maastricht period and put pressure on the Twelve to find adequate responses. In Western Europe itself, the ratification procedure of the Treaty was much more difficult than anticipated. There was strong opposition in many member-states both at the party level and among the wider public. In some cases constitutional changes had to be made before parliaments could ratify the Treaty. From the outset, it was clear that at least in Denmark and Ireland a referendum had to be held (as had previously been the case for the Single European Act).

Besides ratification, the definition of the CFSP, the development of WEU's role in the European security architecture, and the enlargement of the Union, notably towards the EFTA countries, had to be tackled. This last issue had been put aside in Maastricht, but afterwards became more pressing as the number of applicant countries grew. In addition, problems continued in the transatlantic relationship despite the diplomatic language of NATO's Rome summit declaration designed to ease tension over the European defence identity.

Ratification difficulties

The ratification of the Maastricht Treaty revealed the enormous problems involved in deepening integration among the 12 member-states. The fact that Denmark and Britain are the most recalcitrant partners was not all that became obvious. Even in France it was impossible to mobilise strong public support for the Treaty. Consequently, governments will find that their freedom of manoeuvre in future IGCs is more constrained as they keep an eye on both their domestic climate and the conditions which may facilitate parliamentary acceptance.

The negative result of the Danish referendum on 2 June 1992 came as a great shock to Community partners, and also disappointed the Schlueter government which had successfully defended Denmark's interests in negotiations on the Treaty.[1] The Danish electorate was divided almost down the middle on the issue, with only a very small majority voting against the EU project (50.7%). Traditional resistance to the Community becoming a defence union played the same role as scepticism about Europe as a superstate and ill-defined fears of being dominated by a 'powerful', uncontrollable Brussels bureaucracy. Some elements of this criticism also came out in the public debates in other member-states, such as Britain, Germany, Italy and the Netherlands.[2]

Partly in reaction to the events in Denmark, but mainly for domestic reasons, François Mitterrand announced that a referendum would be held in France. After weeks of unprecedented intensive public debate on France and Europe, which turned out to be far more fundamental than the government had expected, the referendum of 20 September 1992 showed only a very small majority (51%) in favour of the Maastricht Treaty. This was in part a result of protest votes against the Mitterrand government, farmers' discontent with the EC's agricultural policy and fears of a German-dominated Union.[3]

The meagre result of the French referendum and the Danish 'no' strengthened those forces within Britain's ruling Conservative Party which opposed deeper European integration. Additionally, the monetary crisis which, in September 1992, led to the withdrawal of the British pound and the Italian lira from the ERM of the EMS, worsened the climate of the British debate on Maastricht. Under these circumstances, Prime Minister Major postponed the third reading of the ratification bill until after the Danish problem had been solved. The bill passed through the House of Commons in July 1993, but only because of a vote of confidence (which left no choice to the dissidents in the Conservative Party other than to accept the Treaty). After the House of Lords had voted positively and the High Court had rejected an accusation against the ratification bill on 2 August 1993, the British government was eager to deposit the ratification document in Rome as quickly as possible.

The second Danish referendum, on 18 May 1993, under a new (social-democratic-led) government produced a majority of 56.8% in favour of the Treaty. This was certainly influenced by the European Council's decision in Edinburgh in December 1992 to grant Denmark exemptions from the Treaty in the areas of defence policy, monetary policy (non-participation in the third stage of EMU), European citizenship and judicial and police affairs.[4] The new and crucial point was the acceptance by the other member-states of Denmark's non-participation in 'decisions and actions of the Union which have defence implications'. In the other areas, the European Council clarified or anticipated only rights which Denmark already had under the Treaty, subject to special protocols or intergovernmental consensus procedures.

By early August 1993, 11 countries had ratified the Maastricht Treaty and it was Germany, ironically one of the strongest promoters of EU, which brought up the rear. Although the Bundestag had voted positively on Maastricht with an overwhelming majority in December 1992, several actions against the Treaty had been brought before the Federal Constitutional Court in Karlsruhe. This delayed progress until October 1993 when Karlsruhe gave the green light by arguing that the Treaty did not limit the constitutional rights of German citizens because the EU was a confederation of sovereign states and not a federation.[5] The Court's view was also influenced by another fact: the Bundestag had amended the fundamental law and established a new Article XXIII committing Germany to the EU and making future changes to the Treaty dependent on a two-thirds parliamentary majority. In addition, the Bundestag, like the Dutch parliament, and in view of widespread German fears that the deutschmark could be sacrificed on the altar of European integration without receiving a stable European currency in exchange, had made agreement on entering the third stage of EMU dependent on parliamentary consent.[6]

The more immediate implications of the ratification debate are:

– The momentum of European integration has been lost and the Treaty weakened. It is increasingly unlikely that the Union can be transformed in the near future into a defence community through the absorption of WEU, not only because of the cautious attitudes of the more Atlantic-oriented member-states and the position of neutral Ireland, but also because of the non-participation of Denmark in defence-related areas of the EU's security policy.

– The Union is not a homogeneous entity. The special regulations for Denmark indicate once more that variable membership may become a general pattern of integration. If Denmark is not forced to follow strictly the spirit of the Maastricht Treaty and parts of its provisions, why should future members not be granted similar exemptions if they face severe ratification problems, even if there is at present a consensus among the Twelve that new members should not have this possibility? However, as long as opting-out is used with care and does not become an excessive rule of the game, it is worth paying the price to keep the integration process moving.

– Tensions between the nation-state and transnational integration have not only continued, they have become stronger. The more integration moves into core areas of national sovereignty, such as currency and defence, the more nation-states resist. This is particularly the case in times of economic recession and severe domestic problems. Whether the agreements of the Edinburgh and Copenhagen summits on more efficient subsidiarity will solve this problem or, instead, serve as a loophole for the renationalisation of certain EC policies remains to be seen.

– Issues of sovereignty and national identity clearly have to be surmounted on the way to deeper integration. Not only will it become more difficult to transfer national competences to Brussels, but the rationality of such a move will have to be better substantiated by governments. The paradox that sovereignty can only be preserved by giving some of it away to Brussels in order to regain it in a collective framework must be explained. Outside the Union, there are only limited opportunities for influencing European affairs and maintaining national welfare. This may well be why the British government tried to ratify the Maastricht Treaty and why other countries applied for membership in the EU.

– The democratic control of integration and the involvement of relevant political forces at an early stage of reforming European institutions have to be ensured. Both the French and Danish referenda demonstrated the gap in confidence between governments and people, something which has to do not only with integration policies, but also with unresolved problems regarding immigrants and refugees, recession and unemployment. Nevertheless, there is growing concern among the citizens of certain member-states that integration policies are a matter of cabinet diplomacy and that decisions on Europe's destiny are far removed from the people. If the integration process fails to take this problem seriously, internal instability and a lack of sufficient democratic legitimation will prevail.

Defining the CFSP

Since the Maastricht summit, foreign ministers have to define the CFSP, but, so far, related work in the EPC framework has made only slow progress. Internal differences on the appropriate responses to the continuing Yugoslav crisis and the long-standing uncertainties over the Maastricht Treaty have all had a negative impact.

On an operational level, however, some new structures have been created which are relevant to the CFSP. A security group, responsible for the conceptual elaboration of the CFSP, has been set up under the auspices of the political directors, and previous regional EPC working groups have been merged with the corresponding EC groups. The EPC Secretariat has become the CFSP unit of the Council's Secretariat and its personnel will be doubled. A group of senior officials of the Twelve has been formed to deal with French Prime Minister Balladur's proposal for a European Stability Pact. Its work provides the basis for one of the first joint actions within the framework of the Union's CFSP. The EC Commission has established a new Directorate-General for 'External Political Relations' (DG-Ia), headed by Commissioner Hans van den Broek, whose task is to enable the Commission to exercise its right of initiative in the CFSP according to the Maastricht Treaty.

On the conceptual side, three reports have been produced: the first on the likely development of the CFSP, presented by the foreign ministers to the European Council in Lisbon (June 1992); the second on the security aspects of the CFSP drawn up by the security group (December 1992); the third drawn up by the same group on European security interests and common principles of the future CFSP (June 1993).[7] All three reflect the embryonic state of definition of the CFSP. They leave many options open and their overall approach to proposals for joint action is cautious since such action requires strict discipline on the part of Union members. They also demonstrate the difficulty of defining common security interests beyond merely adding up the interests of individual member-states.

Based on the conclusion that the causes of conflicts and threats to peace are rooted in economic, political and social instability, all three reports reflect the understanding that the EU's security role is primarily oriented towards addressing these causes. This implies: the strengthening of political, diplomatic and economic ties with neighbouring countries or regions; the use of economic instruments, either in the form of aid and privileged relations with the EC/Union or in exercising pressure on one or more conflicting parties which do not respect the principles of the CSCE and the UN Charter; the promotion of regional cooperation and integration in other parts of Europe and the world as a means of pacifying relations among the states concerned (which is in fact the export of the West European model); and the improvement of the Twelve's instruments for crisis management (monitoring missions, good offices, arbitration, conciliation, peace conferences). Although these deliberations focus on the strategic assets of a civil power, they are based on the assumption that security policy must be founded on a comprehensive concept that includes military aspects. Yet, the full application of such a concept implies close cooperation with WEU, and the reports are unclear about how the division of labour between WEU and the CFSP could work in practice, nor do they define the defence aspects of security or mention compatibility with NATO.

Apart from these general aspects, the second report gives an insight into policy areas in which joint actions could be applied: the CSCE; disarmament and arms control; non-proliferation; and economic aspects of security. Since its inception, the CSCE has always been one of the priorities of the EPC, and the Twelve have largely contributed to adapting it to the post-Cold War situation. Consequently, the second report proposes joint action to strengthen the CSCE. It mentions establishing *ad hoc* steering groups, creating a Secretary-General (which has since been done) and enhancing the presidency. It also suggests that the EU and its member-states could contribute financially or in other forms to CSCE activities.

In the field of arms control and disarmament, joint actions are primarily envisaged for measures discussed in the CSCE Forum for Security Cooperation. Subregional arms control and the code of conduct on politico-military aspects of security are at the forefront of the Twelve's interests here. Nuclear non-proliferation, on the EPC agenda only since the first half of 1990, could become a high-ranking issue for the Twelve. A broad range of possible action is mentioned, including promoting adherence to the Nuclear Non-Proliferation Treaty (NPT); measures to strengthen the International Atomic Energy Agency (IAEA) safeguards regime; the preparation of the NPT review conference in 1995; the prevention of a 'brain drain' of nuclear and other weapons scientists (e.g., through strengthening the science and technology centre in Moscow); and the prevention of ballistic missile proliferation. A common non-proliferation policy would, without doubt, strengthen the NPT regime, particularly if trade concessions or privileged relations with the EC/Union were to be made conditional on adherence to and compliance with the Treaty. Thus at its meeting in Copenhagen in June 1993, the European Council made relations between Ukraine and the EC conditional on Ukraine's ratification of the Strategic Arms Reduction Talks (START I) (including the Lisbon Protocol) and its accession to the NPT as a non-nuclear power.[8]

Turning to economic aspects of security, the second report focuses on weapons transfers. This important aspect of international security is particularly relevant since countries such as Britain, France and Germany are among the ten largest arms exporters in the world. However, the Twelve are still far from a common arms export-control policy even if steps in this direction have been made since the second half of 1991. Yet, the report advocates financial help or advice to developing countries and CSCE states in implementing the UN Register of Conventional Arms and promoting the wider application of the arms exports principles of the Twelve (as proposed within the CSCE Forum for Security Cooperation). Furthermore, the EU envisages a common licence revocation policy and will review the arms-embargo policies of the EC and the UN. These positive proposals notwithstanding, the arms export issue is a good example of the problems the Twelve face in acting as an entity while most of them are reluctant to grant the EU the necessary powers (this would for example require changing or abolishing Art. 223 of the EC Treaty).

In its second report the security group also proposed joint actions for humanitarian missions and the support of UN crisis-management activities, including peacekeeping operations. Unfortunately, deputy political directors did not go into detail here because of the sensitivity of the issue (the report had been elaborated under the Danish presidency). The Union's support of UN activities could include, however, financial contributions or food aid in the same way that the EC has supported work in Bosnia-Herzegovina and Somalia. The EU could also go further by requesting that WEU or member-states contribute militarily to UN operations.

Implications of an EU enlargement to EFTA
The third important issue on the post-Maastricht agenda was the enlargement of the EU, notably to include the EFTA states. In July 1992 the Commission drew up a report which reviewed the cases of applicant countries such as Austria, Finland, Norway, Sweden and Switzerland, as well as Turkey, Malta and Cyprus and Central and East European countries (which, with the exception of Poland and Hungary, have not officially applied, but intend to join the West European club). It pointed out that enlargement is, on the one hand, a challenge to the Union because it affects its efficiency as well as its security and defence dimension and, on the other hand, a chance to shape Europe's political and economic order.[9]

The interests of EU countries in an enlargement to EFTA, notably in view of its security implications, diverge, particularly among London, Bonn and Paris, although a significant *rapprochement* of the three positions has taken place.[10] Britain, once a leading member of EFTA, favours an EFTA enlargement with an eye to integration in the wider Europe and because it sees enlargement as a way of slowing down political deepening. But as regards the neutrals, Britain clearly differentiates between widening EU and WEU membership (so as not to weaken WEU's function as the European pillar of NATO). Germany is in favour of an EFTA enlargement not only because of its geographic position and cultural as well as historic ties with some of these states, but, like other Union members, it is aware that the complexity of decision-making in a Union of 16 members may risk diluting integration; hence, it stresses the need to modify the rules.[11] Neutrality is not seen as a fundamental problem since the countries concerned are willing to change their security concepts. France also has reservations about the institutional impact and, more fundamentally, about implications for the security and defence dimension of the Union. Nevertheless, against the backdrop of the Maastricht Treaty ratification crisis, France's concerns on the defence issue have reduced significantly. Already in autumn 1992, President Mitterrand, together with Chancellor Kohl, strongly supported negotiations with the EFTA countries. Because of the Scandinavian applicants, both leaders counted on the positive impact of this step on the Danish situation.[12]

The Benelux countries shared this view and, because of the strong British interests in the matter, the European Council decided at its meeting in Edinburgh in December 1992 to start official negotiations in February 1993 with Austria, Sweden, Finland and later Norway. This demonstrated the clear shift in priorities from deepening to widening. But negotiations with the EFTA countries could only begin after European leaders found a compromise solution to increasing the Community's financial resources by nearly 25% in 1993–99. Without this budget deal it would have been difficult for Spain, Portugal, Greece and Ireland to board the enlargement train, countries which fear a widening economic gap between them and the richer countries in the centre and the north. This is also why Spain insists that the move towards the third stage of monetary union should be decided by the present 12 EU states to reduce the risk of it becoming detached from monetary integration.

In principle, conditions for integrating the EFTA states into the Union are fairly good. The treaty on the European Economic Area is already turning these countries into 'silent' participants in the EC's single market, even if agriculture and fisheries posed serious problems, above all in the negotiations with Norway. However, the rows over cod quotas and the internal question of the blocking minority in EC decision-making, given the future greater number of countries involved, were somewhat depressing. In contrast, the neutrality of most of the EFTA countries (only Norway is a member of NATO) has not been an obstacle since they have accepted the relevant parts of the Treaty on European Union (which is not a defence alliance). The Commission, which has changed its view on defence, had initially proposed that, with regard to the CFSP, 'specific and binding assurances' should be sought from the neutral EFTA countries. But what kind of assurances could be demanded beyond accepting the wording of Title V of the Maastricht Treaty if the member-states themselves were unable to agree on anything more than aims in the defence-policy fields? Moreover, why should neutral EFTA countries not participate in a CFSP which focuses more on political aspects of security than on defence-related issues?

The concept of neutrality largely lost its rationale at the end of the Cold War and the Swedish, Finnish and Austrian governments have already reduced or modified their concepts of neutrality.[13] For Austria, given its geo-strategic situation, the security dimension of European integration has become its prime motive for seeking accession to the Union. Most neutrals feel more exposed than EU states to potential or acute threats, which gives them an incentive for full participation in the future CFSP and eventually in its defence component (WEU). But, irrespective of what governments think or intend, the notion of neutrality is a deeply rooted domestic affair. The citizens of the countries concerned feel that it is part of their national identity, and opinion polls in Sweden, Finland and Austria show that large parts of the populations are not on the same wave-length as their governments. It will take time to change these self-images and to adapt foreign and security policies to contemporary realities and those of the Union and WEU in particular.

The accession of EFTA countries will strengthen the economic power base of the EU because they have a high per capita income and many already meet the conditions for monetary union. The EFTA countries can thus enhance the Union's ability to support economic development as a stabilising factor in neighbouring regions to the east and the south.

Neutral EFTA states can also enrich the security policies of the Union because they traditionally have diplomatic ties with East European countries and Moscow. Moreover, all the neutrals have long-standing experience of peacekeeping activities. Unlike Germany, Sweden, Austria and Finland would have no problem supporting classic peacekeeping operations under the UN or the CSCE, perhaps in parallel (or in coordination) with WEU.

Irrespective of these positive aspects of enlargement, more or less problematic implications and options for developing the Union and its security and defence dimension remain. Neutral countries, having entered the Union, could tend to stick to their traditional foreign and security policies which would weaken the defence ambitions of the Maastricht Treaty. If enlargement were completed before 1996 (as scheduled), the next round of negotiations on the CFSP provisions of the Treaty would become very complex. However, in the long term, if public opinion in these countries shifts and their security remains less assured than that of the old member-states, countries such as Austria or Finland could strongly support a common defence policy.

Should enlargement to include the neutral EFTA countries fail because of institutional problems or negative referenda results caused by economic difficulties or the defence/neutrality issue, the development of a new European order based on extended integration would be jeopardised and resistance to political deepening could grow. To avoid this the Twelve should pursue a flexible policy. In the case of major ratification problems over the Union Treaty's security dimension, a similar status to that of Denmark could be granted, at least for a transitional period. The problems inherent in a Danish-style solution are clear, but could be reduced if neutral EFTA countries were prepared to accept the *acquis politique* so as not to block decisions on defence aspects of security.[14]

All three neutral EFTA countries, after joining the Union, intend to obtain observer status in WEU and eventually to become members of it.[15] But membership of WEU requires abolishing neutrality, something which is unlikely in the near future (in Austria it would involve changing the constitution). Thus the number of Union countries which are not full members of WEU will increase, making a merger of WEU and the Union in the next coming years less likely and possibly also affecting their close relationship.

NATO membership is another problem. Whereas in Austria, officials tend to ignore or play down WEU's role as the European pillar of NATO, Finnish and Swedish representatives take it into consideration, even if it is perceived as not opportune to join NATO in case it affects relations with Russia.[16] If WEU wishes to maintain its function as NATO's European pillar, membership of it would mean simultaneous accession to NATO. Thus integration *à la* Maastricht would automatically require the enlargement of NATO if new Union states wanted full membership of WEU. However, the issue does not pose any acute problem because neutrals can only become observers in WEU. But this also implies that their security will not be formally guaranteed for some time. It remains to be seen what kind of dynamic results from this and from the possibility of neutral EFTA states making use of NATO's Partnership for Peace (PFP) offer (which has been made to all North Atlantic Cooperation Council (NACC) and CSCE countries). Participation in the PFP programme could give Finland, Sweden and Austria some experience of working with NATO. This may make their subsequent decisions about membership in both defence organisations easier.

The evolution of WEU

In contrast to the problems of defining the CFSP, WEU was relatively successful in implementing the Maastricht declarations, which marks an important change in its functions from previous decades.[17] The different national views of WEU's role – whether primarily oriented towards the Sixteen or the Twelve – prevailed to some extent, but when implementing the Maastricht decisions all member-countries had (and have) an interest in building up the institution and expanding the scope of its work.

WEU has several working groups, including experts and sub- or *ad hoc* groups, which deal with a broad spectrum of day-to-day affairs and mid-term security problems.[18] The topics dealt with are, *inter alia*: cooperation in the verification of the Conventional Armed Forces in Europe Treaty (CFE) or in the implementation of the Open Skies Treaty (where WEU intends to create a pool of observation aircraft); military options in connection with the Yugoslav crisis (prior to and in parallel with successive UNSC Resolutions); and assessment of developments and conflict potential in neighbouring regions to the south and to the east, including the former Soviet Union.

To realise 'a genuine European security and defence identity', member-countries had decided in Maastricht to enlarge WEU to include other EU and European NATO countries and to strengthen its operational role, mainly by creating a 'WEU Planning Cell; closer military cooperation complementary to the Alliance in particular in the fields of logistics, transport, training and strategic surveillance; meetings of WEU Chiefs of Defence Staff; military units answerable to WEU; enhanced cooperation in the field of armaments with the aim of creating a European armaments agency'.[19] They also agreed to transfer the Secretariat and the Council to Brussels and to appoint (new) permanent representatives to WEU.

INSTITUTIONAL AND OPERATIONAL IMPROVEMENTS

Many parts of this programme have already been realised, including the transfer to Brussels (completed in January 1993) and the formation of a new, more professional Council. The official inauguration of a Satellite Centre in Torrejón (Spain) took place in April 1993. The Independent European Programme Group (IEPG), which had previously dealt with West European armaments cooperation, was absorbed by WEU with the intention of creating a European armaments agency.[20] This was made possible by the enlargement of WEU to include other European NATO allies (see below), which also allowed most of the functions of NATO's Eurogroup (in which France had not participated) to be transferred to WEU.

The WEU Planning Cell, with around 30 military officers, became fully operational in April 1993. It has links with the military delegates to WEU and the Chiefs of Defence Staff of the member-countries (who meet twice a year) and is under the direct authority of the Council. Its tasks are to prepare 'contingency plans for the employment of forces under WEU auspices'; to make recommendations for 'command, control and communication arrangements, including standing operating procedures for headquarters which might be selected'; and to keep an updated list of military units 'which might be allocated to WEU for specific operations'.[21]

Some progress has also been made in defining military units for WEU, such as the Eurocorps (fully operational in 1995), the highly mobile NATO multinational division central (in which Belgium, Britain, the Netherlands and Germany participate), and the UK–Netherlands amphibious force.[22] In principle, WEU units will be multinational, drawing on a double-hatting formula by using either national or NATO forces to avoid duplicating what already exists (including double-hatted headquarters). *Ad hoc* arrangements will prevail in crisis situations and no member-state is committed to contribute to operations if it does not wish to do so or if it cannot do so for constitutional reasons. Forces answerable to WEU can be deployed 'apart from contributing to the common defence' of the Alliance for: 'humanitarian and rescue tasks; peacekeeping tasks; tasks of combat forces in crisis management, including peace-making'.[23]

Article VIII of the modified Brussels Treaty allows consultation among member-governments on any event 'which may constitute a threat to peace, in whatever area this threat should arise'. No formal out-of-area problem exists for WEU and the Petersberg Declaration of June 1992 does not mention restrictions on the use of its forces except where this contravenes the principles of the UN Charter. However, peace-making in the sense of peace enforcement by military means, as covered by Chapter VII of the UN Charter, would certainly require a UNSC Resolution. But not all WEU members wish to grant Russia or China a permanent veto on WEU actions and there is an ongoing debate over whether, in certain circumstances, Article 51 of the UN Charter could be used if decisions in the UNSC were blocked (one of the central controversies in Germany). In the field of humanitarian aid or peacekeeping, WEU can act without UN authorisation, even if there is a clear preference for acting under UN or CSCE auspices.

Negotiations on enlarging WEU were concluded by the Rome Council Meeting on 20 November 1992.[24] Since only Greece met the conditions for becoming a full member, debates focused on the rights of observers and associates, both innovations not covered by the modified Brussels Treaty. In the end, member-states agreed that observers (Ireland and Denmark) can attend meetings of the Council and of working groups.[25] Beyond this, associate members (Norway, Iceland and Turkey) have the right to speak, but not to vote because they are also not parties to the WEU Treaty.[26] They will, however, be linked to the Planning Cell and connected to WEU's telecommunication system (WEUCOM) and can take part in WEU military operations on the same basis as full members. The document on association is not legally binding as, for example, Turkey had wished. But WEU members neither wanted to give the impression of extending security guarantees under the modified Brussels Treaty to associates, nor to open a back door for Union membership.

SHORTCOMINGS
The impressive institutional development of WEU contrasts with the deficiencies of its practical policies and military abilities as demonstrated by its meagre contribution to managing the Yugoslav crisis. A variety of factors and events have affected WEU. The dissolution of the Soviet Union lowered the priority given to defence in Western Europe and the new strategic environment highlighted member-states' different security interests and perceptions. The lack of a coherent EC policy towards the Yugoslav crisis also had its impact. Whereas the absence of 'Europe' during the Gulf War led to the call for a stronger operational role for WEU, the Yugoslav experience revealed the practical problems. The fact that NATO might more actively develop peacekeeping capabilities makes it less easy to find appropriate tasks for WEU. Many member-states initially felt that WEU would be the only Western military organisation undertaking missions and operations as defined in the Petersberg Declaration outside the Alliance's treaty area. This changed with NATO's involvement in the Yugoslav crisis and the decisions of its Council at meetings in Oslo and Brussels in June and December 1992 when all 16 member-countries accepted that the Alliance also has a mandate to support peacekeeping activities of the CSCE and the UN.[27]

It has become more difficult to reach a consensus among WEU member-states on when and how it should and could act. Should it undertake atypical activities such as police and customs operations as it currently does on the southern Danube? Germany in particular is interested in such operations as long as it is not expected to participate in military crisis management. This part of the debate has much to do with the military inequality among WEU countries, with Germany towards the bottom of the spectrum and Britain and France, both with long-standing traditions of military intervention and peacekeeping, at the top.

There are other problems which are related to WEU's lack of capacity. Complex military operations require solid command structures and certain assets which only NATO and its strongest member, the US, have at their disposal (including real-time intelligence and big air-lift capacities). Because of its comparative advantage NATO manages the no-fly zone over Bosnia-Herzegovina and is ready to provide air cover for UN forces in the protected areas. This is also why most WEU member-countries want NATO to take responsibility for implementing an eventual peace plan for the former Yugoslavia.

An institution which has just begun to develop its operational capacities should not, however, be judged too critically. More forces and headquarters may become answerable to WEU, exercises will be held in the coming years and some of WEU's structures may be finalised. But member-states are facing difficult choices and most do not want to create redundant capacities or duplicate tasks which NATO already undertakes. It is also unrealistic to develop within only a few years a European space-based observation system to be used for military purposes at a time when member-states face serious budgetary constraints. The armaments agency, which could rationalise and combine member-states' resources, exists only in theory while most countries prefer national solutions for adapting their defence industries to the post-Cold War situation.[28]

It was not by chance, therefore, that WEU ministers, at their meeting in Luxembourg on 22 November 1993, voted unanimously for a strong transatlantic partnership and suggested that WEU should have the possibility of using the 'communication systems, command facilities and headquarters' of the Atlantic Alliance.[29] The details were discussed in consultation with the North Atlantic Council, representing the first important input by WEU members to Allied decision-making. This undoubtedly contributed to the success of the NATO summit on 10 and 11 January 1994 where the Sixteen agreed that 'collective assets of the Alliance' could be made available to WEU and that the concept of Combined Joint Task Forces (CJTF) should be developed to improve cooperation between NATO and WEU and to 'facilitate contingency operations'.[30]

INTER-INSTITUTIONAL COMPLEXITY

The decisions of the Alliance summit, including full acceptance of the emerging European security and defence identity, were overdue because relations between WEU and NATO had proven difficult. Within WEU, member-states disagreed over the organisation's future role and its relations with NATO. Quasi-institutionalised disputes over these issues could not be avoided given that six NATO ambassadors (double-hatted) are present at the WEU's Permanent Council along with special representatives, bilateral ambassadors and officials from capitals. The personnel bias towards NATO – which is even stronger among military delegates who are NATO officers (with the exception of the French and Belgians) – has not made development of WEU's own identity any easier.

Within NATO there was (and still is to some extent) concern about the development of WEU and its activities.[31] Although WEU does not intend to duplicate NATO's permanent and integrated structures, NATO and US officials were watching closely to see how WEU developed its operational dimension. The possibility of introducing joint WEU positions into NATO caused concern as NATO did not wish to be confronted by an inflexible West European position. Additionally, there were worries that WEU had entered the arms-control field – a traditional NATO domain – and had made some diplomatic overtures to the CIS republics on the subject of the ratification of CFE, START and the NPT. NATO was initially unhappy that WEU had created a consultative framework with Central and East European countries in parallel with NACC and that WEU ships operated alongside NATO's small flotilla in the Adriatic to monitor the UN embargo. Finally, there were repeated complaints about 'transparency' in WEU–NATO relations regarding the exchange of documents as promised in WEU's Maastricht Declaration.

Some of these problems were resolved by a WEU document on its working relations with NATO and subsequently by a NATO document on cooperation with WEU (in the summer and autumn of 1992).[32] Since WEU's relocation to Brussels, relations between the two organisations have also improved. Working mechanisms have been established between both secretariats, three joint Council meetings have taken place, the Secretaries-General of both organisations attended each other's ministerial council meetings, a joint NATO–WEU command has been established for *Operation Sharp Guard* in order to enforce the UN embargo in the Adriatic (which has been working quite well) and NATO's military committee has accepted, in that context, responsibilities to the WEU Council. This all occurred before the ideological differences and possibilities of cooperation between the two organisations had been clarified at NATO's January 1994 summit. The agreed new military arrangements, however, create some practical problems and may not be sufficient to reduce the complexity of inter-Alliance relations. First, how the CJTF concept can be implemented and how it will work in practice remain to be seen. Second, coordination of decision-making and military planning will have to be intensified and the role of the American Supreme Allied Commander Europe (SACEUR) will need to be defined if WEU is to use NATO's command structure. Third, a combined WEU–NATO command may not always prove as easy to handle as the Adriatic operation where no combat situation has so far emerged. Moreover, the general and typical fact of the present European–Atlantic security system, that the various decision-making structures and hats (national, NATO, WEU) complicate Western security policies, prevails.

The Eurocorps introduces a further hat (the Franco-German Defence Council).[33] This was not only criticised by NATO and the US, but could also create problems within WEU when it expands to include Spain and other WEU countries. WEU will then be confronted by a core group of member-countries building up a half-way European army outside its structures and without the participation of other important member-states such as Britain. On the other hand, the Eurocorps may be the only way Europe can create more integrated military structures to compensate for the deficiencies of WEU.

Relations between WEU and the EU may not always be smooth either. Whereas its working links with NATO are already quite well established, no such practical steps could be undertaken in relation to WEU's second function until the Union Treaty was in force. It will now take time to gain the same level of cooperation between the secretariats and presidencies of both organisations and to clarify whether the Commission's DG-Ia should have access to WEU documents. In addition, the departmentalisation of European security policy-making will require some coordination among the various bodies involved to avoid duplicating work and to achieve a reasonable degree of efficiency. However, most of the technical problems are solvable, and relations between WEU and the Union do not have to be constructed 'out of the blue'. In the past, the WEU Council had been informed regularly by representatives of the Portuguese, British, Danish (in its role as observer) and Belgian presidencies, and there was also an overlap between EPC and WEU substructures when deputy political directors or their representatives were involved in matters concerning both organisations (this is the case with the almost identical composition of WEU's Special Working Group and the EU's Security Group). Even before the Maastricht Treaty was in force, WEU followed closely the political course of the EPC/EC in all relevant security matters, notably in the case of the Yugoslav crisis. But the more the Union develops its CFSP, the more WEU faces the challenge of truly fulfilling its double function as the pillar of NATO and the military component of the Union.

Finally, what is WEU's place in the collective security system of the UN?[34] Although it has, up to now, acted in conformity with Articles 52 and 53 of the UN Charter (in the Gulf or in the former Yugoslavia), WEU does not see itself as a regional arrangement under Chapter VIII of the Charter. It wants to preserve its autonomy and sees Article 48 as a basis for supporting the UNSC's decisions and activities. However, when WEU members contribute militarily to UN activities – for example, the UN Protection Force (UNPROFOR) in the former Yugoslavia – they prefer to do so in close direct coordination with the UN and not through their regional organisation. Until member-countries are prepared to act more collectively, WEU will be a relatively weak regional partner of the UN.

Much of WEU's future depends on the strategic environment, NATO's further transformation, the UN's performance and the process of European integration itself. Through its institutional build-up WEU has certainly achieved a better profile, and since the European defence identity has been fully appreciated, it no longer stands in the shadow of NATO. But whether WEU will be able to fulfil its function as a military pillar of the Alliance depends on the readiness of member-states to develop WEU's own means and structures and on the political will to act either independently or using NATO's infrastructure and assets in cases where the US is unwilling to participate directly in certain operations.

In its relations with the EU much will depend on the pace of the CFSP's development and the extent to which the Twelve will use the stipulations of Article J.4 of the Union Treaty to bring WEU into play. Whether and when it is integrated into the EU framework is an open question related to EU members' ability to reach a consensus on this issue and on making full membership of the Union and WEU congruent. This will not be easy since, at present, two EU states do not participate fully in the Union's defence arm and since the enlargement policies of both organisations increase the number of countries which are full members in only one of the two, the EU, or in neither of them, as is the case with the WEU associates Turkey and Iceland. Thus WEU is likely to continue to play a role beyond 1996 and perhaps beyond 1998. In the near term, its policies of association, cooperation and dialogue with a growing number of countries, including those in the east and the south (the Maghreb), will make it an important focal point for the security policy of many states. This may not, however, facilitate the coordination of the various security interests involved and the development of common positions in military security policy.

A new transatlantic bargain

In order to assess the implications of European integration for transatlantic relations, it is necessary to distinguish between two different phases in the last four years. The first is characterised by mistrust and mixed feelings on both sides of the Atlantic, including the clashes between the Bush administration and the Socialist government in Paris. The second phase, which culminated in NATO's January 1994 summit, is characterised by the growing acceptance that Europe needs the US and that the latter has an interest in a workable European defence cooperation.

THE PHASE OF MISTRUST AND AMBIVALENCE

The Bush administration perpetuated America's traditional ambivalence towards European integration which has existed since the late 1950s. On the one hand, Americans had some interest in a stronger Europe able to shoulder a considerable part of the Western security burden.[35] On the other, they wanted this neither to harm US economic interests nor to undermine America's leadership in Western security and defence policies. This latter interest always came to the fore when Europe tried to move towards a greater defence identity. The most prominent example of this was the so-called 'Bartholomew letter' sent to West European capitals in February 1991 which expressed American concerns over the negotiations on European defence.[36]

However, ambivalence and mixed feelings also existed in Western Europe which sought greater independence from the US by creating its own security and defence mechanisms, while at the same time preserving US security guarantees and turning to America for leadership in unexpected international crises. Similar to American concern about European developments and policies, many Europeans were suspicious of American motives, fearing an attempt to re-establish US hegemony.

In early 1991 strategic analysts proposed that American policy towards Europe should aim to limit European integration to the economic fields in order to secure US dominance in Western security policy-making.[37] But the Bush administration took a more sophisticated approach. It tried to confine the range and scope of European political and security integration to a level still perceived as compatible with US interests. This implied, on the one hand, a clear preference for limited European defence initiatives within the framework of WEU and, on the other hand, the preservation of NATO as the dominant forum for Western security and defence policies and as an instrument for maintaining US influence in Europe.

Although the Maastricht Treaty contains provisions which coincide with many American interests, as formulated by the Bush administration, such as keeping defence separate from the EC, or the non-subordination of WEU under the European Council,[38] US concerns about specific European developments were still evident throughout 1992. They were related, *inter alia*, to: the enlargement policies of WEU and the EC/Union (notably the non-offer of membership to Turkey); attempts to create a European armaments market (which might protect European defence industries against US competitors); the problem of complementarity between WEU and NATO; and, not least, the Eurocorps. Additionally, some European allies, notably France, had grave differences with the US over NATO's role in European security.[39] Wherever it could, France tried to promote the development of WEU and to block decisions on widening NATO's functions. Moreover, France tried to constrain Germany as much as possible within frameworks of defence cooperation such as WEU and the Eurocorps to prevent it becoming a leading partner of the US. The deterioration in relations between Paris and Washington was particularly marked in the first half of 1992 and, even though France moderated its position regarding NATO in late summer of that year, fundamental divergencies prevailed. However, by the end of 1992 some of the tensions were eased when France finally accepted a wider peacekeeping role for the Alliance and NATO's document on cooperation with WEU, and when it was formally agreed to place the Eurocorps under SACEUR for the Alliance's defence and for certain NATO crisis-management missions.

THE PHASE OF *RAPPROCHEMENT*
The second phase (from the end of 1992 to the present) is characterised by the change from the Bush to the Clinton administration, which shows a greater understanding of the relevance of European integration and its difficulties; the change in the French government which led to greater

34

flexibility in its foreign policy; and the evaporation of any Maastricht euphoria in Western Europe.

The Clinton administration gives priority to domestic issues and economic challenges.[40] It is not only more relaxed *vis-à-vis* European defence cooperation, but even firmly supports the security dimension of European integration, reflecting its interest in a better organised Europe able to contribute significantly to reducing the costs of US global commitments.[41] NATO, in its old form, is no longer the best-suited vehicle for securing US interests in Europe, and the Clinton administration is in favour of transforming it into an organisation which can be used for tasks and missions within a system of cooperative and collective security.

In Europe, interest in maintaining the Alliance with the Americans, albeit in a more balanced form, has grown significantly as difficulties over the Maastricht Treaty and the Yugoslav debacle have weakened confidence in a strong EU with an ambitious CFSP. With the deep cuts in US nuclear arsenals in Europe and the planned reduction in the US military presence to 100,000 or 75,000 troops or even less, many Europeans now fear a US retreat rather than a revival of American hegemony.

In France, even if, under conditions of cohabitation, the new government is broadly in line with President Mitterrand on Maastricht and European integration, the Mitterrand era is coming to an end. The Balladur government wishes to maintain a relatively strong US commitment to Europe in a workable but flexible Alliance with a clear European role.[42] Although the reintegration of France into NATO's military structure is not on the agenda, it has been concluded that the French Defence Minister and Chief of Staff should be present at Alliance meetings dealing with peace-support operations. Since the US itself wishes to limit its engagement in European security and Germany is constrained in its role as a military partner, French interest in improving bilateral relations with other countries, notably Britain, has grown. France's policies can be described as flexible bilateralism and multilateralism, which includes using a variety of organisations like the CFSP/Union, WEU, the Eurocorps, NATO and the UN.[43]

NEW PARTNERSHIP, NEW PROBLEMS?
Although developments in Europe and America have eased tension over ideological issues, divergencies on substance are now closer to the fore. Clashes over bilateral and multilateral trade issues (as witnessed during the General Agreement on Tariffs and Trade (GATT) negotiations) seem more difficult to resolve in an era with no common external threat forcing both sides to seek a compromise and prevent a negative spill-over into the field of security cooperation. Although the Uruguay Round of GATT was concluded successfully, both the US and Europe tend to be inward-looking (at least to focus on regional economic development). The Clinton administration emphasises reconstructing American society and economy and favours

35

fair trade, while European governments are facing a deep recession and increased protectionist pressure. This raises doubts over whether both sides will be able strictly to implement agreed trade liberalisations.[44] In addition, the trade policy arsenals of the US and Europe are now relatively equal, which could easily lead to bilateral and sectoral trade wars until the costs become intolerable for both sides.

Neither the Clinton nor the Bush administration intended to use the Yugoslav crisis to re-establish NATO's primacy or US dominance over European security.[45] Europe took the lead and the US followed some distance behind. While the Bush administration had difficulty accepting Europe's move towards recognising individual Yugoslav republics, the Clinton administration had problems with the Vance–Owen Plan. The transatlantic rift became particularly apparent when, in March 1993, the Clinton administration proposed air strikes against Bosnian Serb positions and lifting the arms embargo against the Bosnian government. Both were strictly opposed by Europe which emphasised humanitarian measures and negotiations. In addition, the Clinton administration was itself split between the Pentagon and the State Department (and even within the State Department) and lacked the support both of Congress and the wider public. The Clinton administration's second initiative, in July–August 1993, was much better prepared and proved face-saving. After hours of debate, most of the European allies (and Canada) agreed that NATO could provide air cover for UNPROFOR in the security zones if so authorised by the UN Secretary-General.[46] Both initiatives revealed the difficulties the US encountered in attempting to exercise leadership when most Europeans preferred a different strategy and where other factors (the UN) beyond the control of the US also played a role. Europe was confronted for the first time since the Second World War with an American administration which was everything but consistent in its policies, which was uncertain about its own proposals and which tended to alter its views within weeks, if not days. Thus Europeans had to learn that nowadays US policies will be less predictable, determined much more than in the past by problems of domestic consensus and changing definitions of American interests.

Although some transatlantic unity has been achieved in connection with NATO's Sarajevo ultimatum of 9 February 1994, it should not be overestimated.[47] First, the French initiated the step, not the Americans, and whether the two will continue to pull on the same rope is an open question. Second, after the Serbs withdraw from around Sarajevo, the US may feel confirmed in its view that it would be better to use air power where necessary than to commit ground troops to Bosnia. Third, US readiness to provide ground forces to implement an eventual peace agreement for Bosnia remains very uncertain. Finally, the US, which is now more involved in efforts to achieve a political solution for Bosnia-Herzegovina, does not seem prepared to follow the logic of European negotiation strategies and objectives.

Despite the encouraging decisions of the January 1994 summit and NATO's success regarding the situation in Sarajevo, NATO is still in an uncomfortable situation. It has lost its traditional enemy, its troop levels have been cut by about half and the relevance of its core function, defence, has diminished. In addition, new tasks in the area of collective security have arisen, challenging NATO's long-term performance. The Alliance must be transformed both to secure collective defence and to develop contributions to collective security without further encouraging renationalisation.[48] Whether this can be done through the new concept of CJTF is difficult to judge. CJTF will give the Alliance greater flexibility for coping with new security problems. Although this is in line with American and French interests, it risks transforming the Alliance into a back-up institution for *ad hoc* coalitions of its larger member-states, thus undermining its multilateral character.

As a result of the January 1994 summit, Europe's role in the Alliance has been more clearly defined and fully accepted. Moreover, President Clinton's words that the 'new security must be founded on Europe's integration' are an appeal to the Europeans to go ahead with their integration, including its security dimension.[49] This may facilitate agreement among both the Atlantic and the continentally oriented factions of WEU and the EU over the extent to which a European security and defence policy should be developed.

However, irrespective of this positive aspect, there are differing interpretations of what really happened on 10–11 January 1994. One is that the Americans are about to tip-toe out of NATO's back door, leaving the Europeans holding a baby which will grow up to become their new security.[50] Another interpretation is that the Americans are pursuing a clever strategy by promoting a European security and defence identity while simultaneously retaining a *droit de regard* on West European policy by embedding WEU more firmly into NATO's structures.[51] The notion of separable, but not separate institutions may fit, to some extent, into this argument.

The truth may, however, lie in between. The US has limited its automatic commitment to Europe to the defence of the Alliance's treaty area. This does not imply that it would simply stand back if there were a major threat to the overall strategic balance in Europe, but it does mean that it does not wish to become necessarily involved in so-called 'minor' conflicts. Factors such as costs, risks and the length of military operations count strongly in an America which is adapting its external commitments to its internal capacities. Consequently Europe's future security now lies in many respects in the hands of the Europeans who must develop the necessary structures and means and, above all, the political will to act accordingly.

The Alliance summit has improved the chances of French participation in NATO/WEU combined activities and the decisions of the Sixteen will also help to compensate for the operational deficits of the Europeans. But, not only does the lack of military capabilities limit the options of the Europeans for independent activities, so does the problem of reaching a consensus. It is still unlikely that West Europeans can agree among themselves on military intervention somewhere in Europe or neighbouring regions should it become necessary. In the field of peacekeeping or humanitarian missions and relief operations, however, Europeans, notably the French and British, will continue to make important contributions. But larger operations in these fields require available, properly trained and equipped troops. As things stand today, Europe would even have difficulty in deploying three brigades for wider peacekeeping missions.[52] Unless this small capability is built up in the near future, Europeans can only act on a limited scale, irrespective of WEU's new role and its potential access to NATO's infrastructure and assets.

In cases where Europe has to rely on NATO assets or command structures, it will have to reach a consensus with the Americans. This would appear difficult should the US hold a different view or fear that commitments under Article 5 of the Washington Treaty could be invoked. The US has also no interest in NATO becoming a cost-free 'lending library' for Europe and may thus expect something in return. Its enduring interest lies in using its NATO troops for operations outside Europe (notably in the Middle East), whether or not Europe agrees. The US may also insist on greater European air and missile defence and on a code of conduct in transatlantic defence trade.[53] Hence the implications of the new WEU–NATO–US relationship, how it will work in practice and whether further adaptations of the Alliance will be required, remain to be seen.

French security experts have already proposed reducing NATO's military integration to ensure greater flexibility and have suggested less US representation in NATO's command.[54] But any further steps in adapting the organisation to the post-Cold War situation, particularly NATO's Supreme Command, have to be considered carefully. An American in that post symbolises US defence commitments and security guarantees to NATO members which are of overriding importance while European defence structures remain weak. Since Europe is still a long way from a common defence policy, not to mention a common defence, the essential elements of NATO's structures, and of the US role in it, have to be preserved.

Most West Europeans want the Americans to continue their nuclear guarantee and maintain a certain combined conventional and nuclear presence in Europe unless integration politics lead to a common nuclear strategy, an issue raised by President Mitterrand in January 1992.[55] However, in view of the deterrence concepts of France and Britain such a far-reaching step is highly speculative and it was not by chance that the whole question was omitted from negotiations on the CFSP and WEU's role.

Besides the fact that West Europeans are dependent on certain NATO and US strategic assets,[56] an American troop presence (at whatever level) can help to balance internal West European rivalries and to prevent a greater renationalisation of defence policies, notably if NATO's integrated structures remain unchanged. More than purely an alliance, NATO has developed an important culture of multilateral consultation and cooperation among 16 nations and is still the only institution linking the US and Western Europe in a security community.

A truly balanced transatlantic security community would require NATO's transformation into a structure with two equally strong pillars. But since the preconditions for such a transformation do not exist, Europe and America will have to live with a second-best system of closely interwoven Atlantic and European structures. Assessments of the relevance of potential risks and crises may also differ on both sides of the Atlantic. With no common threat, different geopolitical and geostrategic interests in Europe and America play a much greater role than they did during the Cold War. As a superpower, the US has global interests, whereas Europe has regional interests and is affected much more by conflicts in its direct neighbourhood. But what complicates transatlantic security cooperation more is the different analyses of security problems and the resulting preferences for ways and means of coping with them. Hence, counter-productive policies on either side cannot always be avoided nor can common responses always perfectly be designed to translate into practice those interests which West Europeans and Americans share: limiting conflicts; furthering democracy and human rights; containing an expansionist Russia and integrating it into the world economy; supporting transformations in Central and Eastern Europe; managing global economic interdependence; and preventing arms proliferation.[57]

Conclusions

Three conclusions emerge from this chapter. First, the transatlantic relationship, which has improved since the NATO summit in January 1994, will remain problematic in both the economic and security fields. This is because the post-Cold War interests of a Europe bound by its regional problems and an America with a Russia-centric policy, a growing orientation towards the Pacific region and non-Europeanists in its present administration are increasingly diverging. Much also depends on the Franco-American relationship. Its ups and downs may well continue, even if both countries showed an unanticipated degree of cooperation in the case of NATO's Sarajevo ultimatum and although the new flexibility of Allied military structures is in the interests of France as well as the United States. Any further reform of the Alliance has to be carefully thought through to preserve its core functions and structures and its multilateral character, something which is of paramount interest to member-states such as Germany.[58]

A new transatlantic partnership should also embrace political and economic issues of mutual concern to prevent contradictory developments between these areas and that of security. This implies closer coordination between the EU and the US administration. The basis for this has already been established in the transatlantic declaration of 1990 which now has to be intensified and enlarged, perhaps in the form of an Atlantic Charter as suggested by the German Foreign Minister, Klaus Kinkel.[59]

The Americans are ready to facilitate a stronger European role within the Alliance, but will they always be prepared to give the Europeans political and military support when they need it in certain crises outside the Alliance? Will the West Europeans, who are concentrating much of their energy on integration, be sufficiently aware of the implications of their new security role and of their growing responsibility for a workable transatlantic relationship?

The second conclusion is that, obviously, the construction of Europe still has a very long way to go. Following the difficulties of the ratification procedure, the objectives of the Maastricht Treaty cannot be realised in a strict sense. Factors such as democratic legitimation and the preservation of national identity play an important role in European integration and variable membership in common institutions may become a more prominent feature, particularly in view of enlarging the Union to include the EFTA countries. Decision-making among a greater number of Union countries will also be difficult. If decision-making is not to be watered down, the rules have to be adapted, and controversies over the widening/deepening issue will become more intense. Moreover, the enlargement policies of both WEU and the Union raise the issue of whether they can cooperate smoothly and make the integration of defence into the Union's framework less likely in the near term. Although WEU has gained in stature through its improved institutional and operational elements, many of its functions exist only on paper and a lack of substance has to be overcome in order for it to fulfil its role as a pillar of NATO and the military arm of the Union.

The third conclusion is that the CFSP has only been developed to a very moderate degree. Beyond generalities on the possibility of using the economic and political assets of the Union, only a few areas of security policy have been defined more precisely. The Union would in theory be best suited to play a major role in European and international security, including contributing to conflict prevention and crisis management. The question is whether Union members are willing to make use of the full capacities of the Union and WEU. This requires a consensus on common interests and objectives, something which is hard to achieve in an era in which the identity of security interests cannot be taken for granted.

III. THE TWELVE AND THE WIDER EUROPE

With the end of the Cold War, the European security system faces three basic problems. The first concerns the asymmetry of security structures. Whereas Western Europe has a tight, multilayered security system (NATO, WEU, the EU), Central and Eastern Europe lack comparable structures. As the CSCE cannot offer a reliable alternative, these countries want to strengthen their ties with Western security organisations and eventually become members of them. The second problem relates to the fragmentation of security along subregional lines (the Baltic area, the CIS, Central Eastern Europe, the Balkans, the Mediterranean) and between the eastern and western parts of the continent. While the West European strategic situation is fairly comfortable, that of Central and Eastern Europe is fragile and exposed to various risks. Until summer 1991, fear that Soviet imperialism would be revived preoccupied Central and East Europeans. Since the dissolution of the Soviet Union, it is the developments in Russia and the CIS which make them feel insecure, notably Poland and the Baltic states. The third problem results from the end of Soviet domination over Eastern Europe which freed various centrifugal forces threatening domestic and subregional stability. Nationalism, secessionism and ethnic strife create acute or potential conflicts. The break-up of the Czechoslovakian federation (albeit peacefully), tensions between Hungary and its neighbours, and the never-ending war in the former Yugoslavia, demonstrate the revival of old patterns of Central and East European history.[1] The 'new' types of conflict pose a major problem for a European security system. The classical instruments of Western security policy, efficient in the face of the Soviet threat, are no longer very useful and the development of new means for dealing with conflicts in post-Cold War Europe is still in its infancy.

Whereas the West tended to practise a 'wait-and-see' policy towards Eastern Europe, the Yugoslav crisis and the consequences of the collapse of the Soviet Union have forced it to react. In the former Yugoslavia, the West concentrated its activities on peacekeeping and humanitarian measures. In the former Soviet Union, the control of nuclear weapons, the danger of proliferation and the difficulty of ratifying and implementing arms-control agreements (CFE, START I, the NPT) have become of direct concern to the West. In addition there are now new worries about Russia's policies towards its 'near-abroad', in particular the question of cooperation and conflict between Russia and Ukraine and the risk that the latter could break up. Inter-state as well as intra-state conflicts have already broken out in the southern parts of the former Soviet Union and what might happen if the issue of Russian minorities were to form the background for greater conflicts in the CIS is scarcely imaginable.

The Twelve are only a part of a much larger Europe and the stabilisation of Central and Eastern Europe is one of their prime responsibilities. As the regional differentiation and geopolitical interests of West European countries have become more relevant after the Cold War, their efforts to formulate effective responses and maintain unity of action have been greatly complicated.

Crisis management – the Yugoslav experience

The Yugoslav crisis, even more than the Gulf War, is generally seen as a test of Europe's ability to export security and consequently there is the widespread feeling that Europe cannot fulfil its international responsibilities successfully.[2] The issue is, however, far more complex than front-page newspaper articles might suggest.[3] Europe as a political entity did not exist when the crisis began, and foreign-policy coordination among EC member-states in the framework of the EPC had been developed to deal with external problems of secondary importance, not with high politics or questions of war and peace.

However, Community institutions, and WEU, at least provided a common framework for decision-making and taking action, thus preventing a return to the classical power and alliance policies of major West European players towards the Balkans. Below this general institutional level, however, old rivalries among member-states and different perceptions of each others' intentions came to the surface and hampered any effective approach to the crisis. Britain and France had good relations with Belgrade dating back to the end of the First World War and both were interested in maintaining the status quo.[4] Germany, traditionally close to Slovenia and Croatia (not least because of its large numbers of guest workers from the north of the former Yugoslavia), already demonstrated its preference for recognising the two republics in July 1991. The question of recognition became highly relevant in Germany's Yugoslav politics because of the lack of any other instruments, the principle of self-determination in German foreign policy, and strong domestic pressure for the internationalisation of the conflict.[5] The Community environment restrained the German government from taking any unilateral steps for many months. But when the situation in Croatia worsened with the destruction of Vukovar and the Serbian attacks against Dubrovnik, the Germans increased pressure on their EC partners who finally gave in and agreed to recognise individual republics following general guidelines and a timetable in the case of Slovenia and Croatia.[6] The decision, taken on 23 December 1991 by the Kohl cabinet, to recognise both republics, but not to establish diplomatic relations before 15 January 1992 was thus rather unnecessary. Moreover, it had the counter-productive effect of feeding negative perceptions of the new Germany in France, Britain and other partner countries.

INCONSISTENT AND INADEQUATE POLICIES

Notwithstanding the enormous creativity of the Twelve in establishing diplomatic instruments during the crisis, most measures, and the way in which they were applied, proved inadequate. They came either too late or were too half-hearted.[7] Politically, the Twelve could not play the neutral arbitrator while they favoured maintaining some form of Yugoslavia and, later, when they applied economic sanctions against Serbia and Montenegro. The recognition of entities during a process of conflictual secession proved to be very ambiguous. In the case of eastern Croatia, it helped to end the fighting; in the case of Bosnia-Herzegovina, recognition was followed by an escalation of the conflict. The principles for recognition had not been followed strictly and France was the only country to emphasise that, in view of insufficient minority rights, the recognition of Croatia was conditional. Macedonia, although it has met most of the criteria demanded by the Twelve, has not been recognised collectively because of Greek resistance. Greece's unilateral blockade of Macedonia, aiming at forcing it to change its name and amend parts of its constitution, has put enormous strain on the Twelve.

Economic sanctions were also applied, but it took months to gather the necessary international support through the UN and approximately one year to increase the effectiveness of the sanctions and the arms embargo through tighter land and sea controls. Whereas sanctions are only directed against Serbia and Montenegro, the arms embargo applies to the whole of the former Yugoslavia, thus affecting the strong and the weak in the same way. The organisation of a peace conference was also ineffectual. While the Twelve were neither willing nor able to pressure all parties to agree on a negotiated solution, the conference became a time-saving exercise for those still trying to realise their war aims.

The military options had already been reduced at an early stage (August–September 1991) when the Twelve could not agree on a Franco–German initiative for a WEU interposition force in Croatia, notably because of British resistance.[8] Britain was reluctant to become involved in the Balkans and its experience in Northern Ireland only served to strengthen its concerns. It was also suspicious of the Franco-German initiative because, at that time, there was no agreement on the role of WEU and its relation to the Union in the framework of the IGC on political union. When Germany realised it would be unable to commit any forces, it quickly withdrew from the proposal. Even if the Twelve (and the Nine) had been able to agree on sending a peacekeeping force to Croatia, they would not have obtained the consent of both warring parties because the still-existing federal Yugoslav authorities did not want a WEU presence. In October–November 1991 the Twelve turned to the UN and accepted the primacy of the UN in decision-making for the military management of the crisis. Moreover, they preferred the UN to take full responsibility for all military operations on the ground in the former Yugoslavia. Since emphasis was placed on protection forces other military options were ruled out because of the contradiction between humanitarian measures and enforcement actions on a larger scale (the latter would have required either very strong protection of UN forces or their withdrawal).

The weakness of Western Europe's responses to the crisis may have resulted from an underestimation of Serbian and Croatian intentions, as well as the brutality with which they would be realised. When the war escalated in summer 1992, and the military siege of Sarajevo, the existence of concentration camps and the policy of ethnic cleansing became well known, European governments either completely over-estimated the effectiveness of the measures applied, including those of the UN, or else regarded them, from a more or less cynical, real-political point of view, as an alibi for not doing more. This only changed to some extent after the shelling of Sarajevo's market-place on 5 February 1994. France, responding to strong public pressure, deemed it necessary to initiate a more decisive Western response and, together with the Americans, launched the proposal for NATO's Sarajevo ultimatum. The Bosnian Serbs finally complied with NATO's requirements, but only after Russian diplomatic intervention which convinced the Serbs to defer to the terms of the NATO ultimatum while at the same time reassuring them that, with the despatch of Russian peacekeepers from eastern Croatia to Sarajevo, the Bosnian Muslims would be unable to exploit a Serbian retreat. As a consequence, Sarajevo became a truly safe area, and the Bosnian Serbs intensified their military pressure on Tuzla and elsewhere.

IMPLICATIONS AND LESSONS
As a result of Western Europe's policies towards the Yugoslav crisis the UN became involved, WEU and NATO played their respective roles in supporting or enforcing UN Resolutions, the conflict did not spread and humanitarian measures mitigated some of the suffering of the population in Bosnia-Herzegovina.[9] But the Europeans clearly failed, first, to prevent an escalation of, and then to end, the conflict. They were also unable to take the longer-term implications of politics for the moment into account. Every UN Resolution supported by the Europeans dragged another in its wake, leading to deeper involvement in the crisis. The Twelve also had enormous difficulty overcoming their traditional way of thinking about Yugoslavia, rooted more in the past than in the present. Thus they neglected the objectives of the Maastricht Treaty and the need to take more decisive action earlier to contribute to European security at large. As a result, the former Yugoslavia may become either Europe's Lebanon or a subregion with long-lasting tensions and the constant risk of war between a greater Serbia and a *de facto* greater Croatia – a scenario which the Vance–Owen Plan had tried to avoid. Military intervention for peacemaking purposes was never sug-

gested for very good reasons. First, the crisis did not pose a threat to the overall strategic balance in Europe. Second, the West Europeans were reluctant to undertake larger ground operations because of their realistic fear of becoming involved in an Afghanistan-type conflict, and no politician wished to sacrifice the lives of his country's soldiers on moral grounds alone.

Some argued, purely from the moral point of view, that the Bosnian Muslims should be able to obtain arms from the outside to defend themselves better; others suggested that using airpower against major Bosnian Serb military positions and supply lines could at least limit Serbian operational freedom of manoeuvre. In the event, neither of these options were taken up. All that Europe, together with the US, was able to do with respect to air power was to give NATO the task of enforcing the no-fly zone over Bosnia-Herzegovina (which led to the shooting down of four, probably Bosnian Serb, fixed-wing aircraft on 28 February 1994) and to threaten NATO airstrikes against Bosnian Serb heavy weapons should these not be withdrawn outside a 20-km-zone around Sarajevo within ten days. Thanks to this firm Western stance and Russian diplomacy, NATO did not need to take action in that case and the breakthrough in Sarajevo marked a turning-point in the management of the crisis by adding some military strength to political intervention. Since then the US and Russia have become more deeply involved diplomatically which may facilitate approaching an overall settlement for Bosnia because it is practically impossible to achieve workable compromises between the Bosnian Serbs and Muslims without the more constructive and direct influence of their respective strongest external 'allies'.

The former Yugoslavia will remain on the Twelve's agenda and continue to put strain on them. Should there ever be a workable settlement of the crisis, the EU would be hard pressed not to support individual republics and Western Europe will find itself paying for the reconstruction of the former Yugoslavia. But, more fundamental questions have to be addressed in the longer term. Should most of the former Yugoslavia be isolated, or should formal ties be strengthened, step by step, between individual republics and the EC/Union (as has already occurred in the case of Slovenia)? How should Serbia be treated in the longer run given the principle that borders cannot be changed by force? What should be done with Croatia? New states in which democratic and pluralistic governments have been elected, where the rule of law has been established and where the protection of human and minority rights is secured (if ever) cannot be excluded from European integration. Cooperation and association agreements will have to be offered at some stage and membership may be considered later. What would then be the implications for the internal cohesion of the Union and the prospects of a CFSP given a certain pro-Serbian or certain pro-Croatian and Bosnian Muslim bias of major West European powers?

Apart from these long-term problems, there are more immediate ones for the development of a common security policy. Britain and France play a leading role among both the Twelve and the Nine in all areas of military crisis management. Both countries commit relatively large numbers of troops to UNPROFOR (around 2,000 for the UK and more than 6,500 in the case of France) and their permanent seats on the UNSC strengthen their position. Thus the UN has a constraining effect on a common security policy.[10] This not only underlines the inequality among West Europeans, but also increases the trend towards renationalising security policies. Although West Europeans themselves brought the UN into the Yugoslav crisis, coordination between the Twelve and the UN has not always been smooth. On 10 May 1993, for example, EC foreign ministers agreed to continue to support the Vance–Owen Plan. However, only 12 days later (after the Bosnian Serbs had rejected the Plan), the two permanent European members of the UNSC, plus Spain as a regular member, agreed in Washington with the US and Russia on a new action plan. They did so without prior consultation with the rest of the Twelve, which particularly angered Germany, Italy and the Netherlands. Instead of insisting on tighter coordination between the Twelve and the UN, Germany is now seeking permanent membership of the UNSC to avoid being marginalised in the long run. Thus the importance of the UN is hampering the development of a common military security policy to the extent that it stresses the relevance of great powers.

The autonomy of the Union and WEU in military crisis management is additionally affected by the limited circumstances under which they can act without UNSC authorisation. One possibility, for example, is to act on the basis of Article 51 of the UN Charter which gives the right to assist a third country that has been attacked, even if no formal alliance exists. Whether member-states would agree on this is questionable. Second, due to the types of conflict in Europe and beyond, it might be very difficult to define a situation clearly as an attack by a hostile country against a UN member-state. Nevertheless, the development of a common security policy will remain an important subject on the West European agenda, given alone the need to strengthen links between West European institutions and the UN. The future of the UN is unknown; but it is already clear that it must cooperate with regional groupings of all kinds, which inderlines, in contrast to the above-mentioned trends, the relevance of the Union, WEU and NATO.[11]

The Yugoslav experience has also shown that West European interests diverge particularly strongly in times of acute crisis. One way of avoiding strain among the Twelve is to develop appropriate instruments for preventive diplomacy. These should include a capacity for common risk analysis in the framework of the CFSP and the development of far-sighted strategies to be implemented long before a conflict escalates to a military dimension.

Despite the widespread impression that WEU was playing a zero-sum game *vis-à-vis* NATO, the reality is different, even if there was, for a while, some rivalry between the two organisations over which would contribute to crisis management. But, NATO is currently in a better position regarding the former Yugoslavia. WEU adapted its role to the post-Cold War situation earlier than NATO, when in June 1992, in the Petersberg Declaration, WEU member-countries declared their willingness to support the crisis-management and peacekeeping activities of both the UN and the CSCE.[12] However, WEU only became involved in strengthening the UN embargo by dispatching ships to the Adriatic (first for monitoring and then for enforcement purposes) and through a police and customs operation to support the Danube Riparian States in implementing UNSC Resolution 820 (which involves 300 policemen and customs officers and 12 patrol boats). In contrast, NATO provides the mobile headquarters of NORTHAG to UNPROFOR, conducts *Operation Deny Flight* over Bosnia-Herzegovina, provides the back-bone of the operation in the Adriatic, is responsible for UNPROFOR's air cover in the security zones, made plans for the implementation of the Vance–Owen Plan, and is doing so for an eventual peace agreement.

Whether NATO's peacekeeping planning will come into effect depends on the final parameters of a peace agreement, the readiness of the US to participate and the clarification of arrangements between NATO and the UN. Until now, the Americans have committed only a limited number of troops to UN operations in the former Yugoslavia (around 300 for UNPROFOR III in Macedonia) and have not been continuously involved in the naval operations in the Adriatic. Because of this, WEU is concerned to make its role more visible and many member-countries believe that a variety of ground and sea operations could be carried out entirely under a WEU hat, if NATO's infra- and command structures could be used. However, even the bigger WEU countries, like France and Britain, are at the limits of their abilities to provide more troops for peacekeeping missions. More forces from NATO countries would then be required and without the Americans no global peace plan for Bosnia-Herzegovina could be implemented. The crisis-management capabilities of both NATO and WEU will remain limited as long as neither the US nor Germany participate.

The transatlantic row in 1993 over the correct approach to the Bosnian crisis was, on the one hand, very specific but, on the other, was a general indication of the post-Cold War continental drift between Europe and America. There was little disagreement between the major West European powers and the US over not intervening militarily. Nor did they disagree over the need to contain the crisis and prevent the direct involvement of NATO countries such as Greece or Turkey. But, in contrast to the Europeans, the Americans were obviously interested in changing the management of the crisis by exerting military pressure on the Bosnian Serbs. The

Europeans, notably the British and the French, traditionally used the fact of their *in situ* ground troops to block or water down the American proposals. They wanted neither to risk the lives of their UN forces nor to switch from humanitarian activities to air intervention while prospects on the ground remained uncertain. The outcome of these intra-Western differences was that the Bosnian Muslims felt weakened, the Serbs strengthened and the Croats encouraged. However, the impact on transatlantic relations was that the Americans felt rebuffed and were no closer than the Europeans to finding a solution to the crisis.

That situation changed with NATO's Sarajevo ultimatum. The French dropped their concerns over their UN forces and the Americans pushed the British to agree with NATO's initiative. Evidently the West can act in a cohesive and more decisive way through NATO if the French and Americans are on the same wavelength. As a result the Americans felt more committed to the diplomatic process, but this does not mean that all transatlantic differences over Bosnia have disappeared. The US has its own ideas for influencing developments and its policy is based on supporting constellations which could create a better balance of military power in the former Yugoslavia and which may also help to reduce the number of forces required to implement a possible peace plan for Bosnia. If the US-brokered federation between Bosnian Croats and Bosnian Muslims works, the situation in Bosnia would change considerably and the chances of achieving a compromise with the Serbs, because of stronger internal and external pressures, could increase. At the same time, however, the risk of a war of revenge should the Serbs not be ready to make concessions may grow. This risk can hopefully be kept to a minimum. But US and European views on an overall settlement of the crisis need to be further harmonised to ensure an effective common approach. One thing at least is clear: should a Croat–Bosnian confederation (minus the Bosnian Serbs) become reality, Europeans will have no choice other than to accept the partition of Bosnia-Herzegovina. This would not mean, however, that the EU's action plan of November 1993 (based on the Kinkel–Juppé initiative) would be completely outdated. A comprehensive solution to the crisis in the former Yugoslavia can only be reached in stages and would have to include a determination of the ultimate status of eastern Croatian territories and the safeguarding of minority rights in Kosovo, Sandjak and Vojvodina.

The implications of the Yugoslav crisis for relations with Russia are also ambivalent. Europe has clearly taken Moscow's interests into account in order not to weaken the position of the Russian reform-oriented forces and not to lose Russia as a reliable partner in the UNSC. On the other hand, Russia has become a constraining factor on the activities of the Twelve and WEU. Moreover, the purely verbal condemnation of ethnic cleansing and of the politics of building a greater Serbia by force (and a greater Croatia as well) did nothing to discourage conservatives and nationalists in their ambitions for a greater Russia. The Europeans also neglected the emergence of a stronger axis between Moscow and Belgrade which led to direct Russian involvement in reaction to NATO's ultimatum. With Russian peacekeepers now present in Sarajevo, Moscow will play an important part in achieving a global cease-fire and a political settlement of the Bosnian crisis. This is certainly positive as long as the Russians make constructive use of their special relationship with Serbia and maintain their strategic partnership with the US. Europeans may thus have to work hard to avoid the main parameters for future order in the former Yugoslavia, right in the EU's backyard, being determined largely by these two major powers.

The Yugoslav crisis increased the security dilemma for those states not integrated into tight security structures. Central and East European countries learnt that they could not count on Western assistance, notably if fighting should break out in connection with minority problems. They themselves would have to take responsibility, in the first instance, for their own security. However, their desire to join NATO, WEU and the Union has been strengthened at the same time, and this explains in part why, in spite of some concerns, the Danube Riparian States agreed to cooperate with WEU to make the UN embargo more effective and why they tried to obtain security guarantees in that context.[13] On the other hand, Western Europe's need to develop political instruments such as the European Stability Pact (see below) to help to settle minority and border problems before Central and East European countries can participate more fully in European integration has also become more apparent.

Finally, Western Europe's handling of the Yugoslav crisis has an impact on its relations with the Islamic world. The complication of official relations between Western Europe and Muslim countries is not the major problem; more problematic is the effect of the Bosnian drama on Islamic fundamentalists.[14] By exploiting the issue in their anti-Western policies they weaken the position of the more moderate forces and put strain on the governments of Muslim countries. The potential consequences of these internal mechanisms in the Islamic world have, up to now, been completely neglected, which could well harm Western Europe's longer-term interests in the stability of the Mediterranean.

Security through integration

There are two basic options for expanding the Western stability zone eastwards: to offer security guarantees and membership in Western security institutions; or to integrate the countries concerned step-by-step into the EU. The latter refers to the successful model of security through integration developed between West European states within the last four decades. Both options are complementary rather than mutually exclusive. The post-Second World War history of Western Europe in particular demonstrates that economic and political integration can largely profit from the existence of an overarching security system.

THE ROLE OF NATO AND WEU

Both NATO and WEU have developed cooperative security relations with East European countries below the threshold of membership and formal security guarantees.[15] NACC was established in December 1991 andWEU founded its Forum of Consultation in June 1992.[16] But the enlargement of NACC to include the Central Asian republics of the former Soviet Union turned it into a somewhat heterogeneous body in which Central and East Europeans have difficulty making their specific interests heard. WEU, on the other hand, concentrates on nine Central and East European countries (Bulgaria, Estonia, Hungary, Latvia, Lithuania, Poland, Romania, the Czech Republic and Slovakia). It attaches great importance to relations with these partners in the wider context of European integration. However, many Central and East European countries were disappointed by the degree of cooperation within WEU's Forum of Consultation as well as within NACC and articulated repeatedly their interest in belonging to the Western club and obtaining security guarantees.

The debate on enlarging Western security institutions, notably NATO, also received fresh impetus in 1993 through a variety of contributions from Western academics and officials.[17] German government officials (notably Defence Minister Rühe) spoke most clearly in favour of extending the Western stability zone eastwards. But, even before the NATO summit in January 1994, it became clear that formal expansion of the Alliance would not take place in the near term. The inclusion of a number of new members could, of course, dilute security guarantees and defence commitments. No West European country wishes such an outcome, not least because Western guarantees give Germany the option of maintaining its non-nuclear status. Hence, an eastern expansion of NATO (if not a two- or even three-tier NATO) would require tight security guarantees, including the eventual deployment of Western forces to countries close to the Russian/CIS borders. Most Western governments are not prepared to go so far and the US here faces its greatest obstacle to extending its nuclear guarantees.

Russia's attitude has also influenced Western thinking. Expansion could make Russia feel threatened or, at least, isolated and any enlargement of NATO to include the countries of Central and Eastern Europe would certainly strengthen Russia's conservative–nationalist forces. This will affect the Western debate as long as nobody in a responsible position thinks of materialising the 'victory' of the Cold War by extending NATO's treaty area to the east. Aside from Russia, the more immediate threats to stability in Central and Eastern Europe are internal, stemming from political imbalances, border disputes or minority conflicts. A defence organisation such as NATO is certainly not best suited to handling such issues.

Most of these arguments also apply to the eastern enlargement of WEU, which has even more binding treaty obligations than NATO. Moreover, the full members of WEU form an inner circle of the Sixteen and the Twelve. Allowing Central Europeans to join the WEU Treaty now would imply abandoning the Maastricht doctrine by detaching WEU from its function as the European pillar of the Alliance and the defence component of the EU.

Against this background, both NATO and WEU tried to find an interim solution to their dilemma. NATO, on the basis of an American proposal, has already offered PFP agreements to all NACC members and other CSCE countries.[18] Although no security guarantees are linked to the PFP agreements, consultations are envisaged for participants who feel that their security or territorial integrity is threatened – without, however, indicating what that might imply in practice. PFP also offers closer ties to NATO's political and military bodies outside its ordinary structures through permanent liaison officers and the planned coordination cell at SHAPE in Mons. Finally, PFP provides for joint military planning, exercises and cooperation with NATO in peacekeeping, as well as search, rescue and humanitarian operations.

NATO's initiative has been greatly appreciated by countries which feel relatively insecure, such as the three Baltic states and Albania. Other Central European states, such as Poland, accepted NATO's offer more reluctantly because neither a timetable nor criteria for accession to NATO have been put forward. With PFP, NATO is doing exactly the opposite of what the Central and East European countries want: making a clear distinction between their case and other NACC countries from the CIS region, notably Russia. Moreover, the possibility of so-called 'self-differentiation' in the concrete shape of individual partnership agreements may further rivalry among Central European countries in their race for future membership of NATO.

PFP does not envisage a specific role for Russia, nor does it cover the issue of peacekeeping in the CIS as a matter of collective security.[19] Although Russia may be pleased that no decision on NATO's formal expansion has been made, it was not unduly enthusiastic about the PFP offer. Russia is interested in strengthening the CSCE and linking NACC to it. Most of all, Russia wishes an upgrading of NACC *vis-à-vis* NATO, with an important role for itself within the NACC framework. The relationship between NACC and the CSCE, however, remains largely undefined, and deepening relations between individual countries and NATO may weaken the multilateral character of NACC.

Dissatisfied with NATO's PFP offer, many Central and East European countries are concentrating on closer relations with WEU which is considering introducing an 'enhanced status' for Consultation partners. The conclusions of the WEU Council on 22 November 1993 reflected a joint Franco-German proposal for associating those Central European countries to WEU which have Euro-agreements with the EC.[20] Enhanced status (which is also favoured by Britain) will not be linked to any security guarantee and will have to be different from that of associate members of WEU. But it would indicate that WEU takes the security concerns of Central European countries seriously and that these countries would be more involved in WEU's own structures, which would thus move essentially closer to their basic interests. However, a formalised relationship will also need to be complemented by adding more substance to practical cooperation in areas such as peacekeeping, verification of arms-control agreements and CSCE matters. To substantiate an enhanced relationship with Central European partners will be a challenge for WEU which is still busy developing closer cooperation and greater cohesion amongst its own members.

THE EUROPEAN STABILITY PACT

Another initiative for dealing with security problems in Central and Eastern Europe is the Twelve's European Stability Pact. When the idea was launched in spring 1993 by French Prime Minister Balladur, it stemmed largely from the new right-wing government's intention to exercise some influence over French foreign policy and not leave it exclusively to the Socialist President. The proposal also had to do with the Yugoslav experience and concerns about potential ethnic and territorial disputes between Central and East European countries which have close ties with the EC/Union and wish to join the West European club. Finally, France wanted to give its eastern policies a better profile because it opposed the speedy eastward expansion of both NATO and the Union.

The Balladur Plan, proposed as an exercise in preventive diplomacy,[21] had many deficiencies and was strongly criticised in Central Europe but also in Western Europe.[22] Criticism was directed at the issue of making membership of the EU conditional on signing the Stability Pact; the issue of the Pact's guarantees; the relatively late involvement of major powers, like the US; the relationship between the CSCE and a large conference project dealing with CSCE principles; and the fact that 'minor rectification of borders' was not ruled out in the French proposal.

The Twelve, however, attached great importance to the idea and developed it into a joint action of the CFSP. A high-level group has been formed to prepare the project; consultations have begun with those countries on which the proposal is focused; and the US has been kept informed. A first readjusted plan was adopted in December 1993,[23] aiming at a three-phased process with an inaugural conference in Paris (probably to be held in May 1994), round-tables for negotiating bilateral treaties covering minority and border problems, and the approval of agreements by all participating states. The negotiation process will focus on the six Central European EC associates, the three Baltic states and Slovenia, but will also involve the US,

Russia and other countries bordering the Central European region to the north, the east and the south (excluding most of the republics of the former Yugoslavia) and representatives of the relevant international institutions (CSCE, WEU, NATO, UN). In contrast to the Balladur proposal, the Union's plan did not mention territorial revisions. Instead, the 'consolidation of borders' was stressed. The EU also reduced its role to that of a catalyst and it was suggested that bilateral agreements should be supervised by the CSCE 'as a guardian' of the Stability Pact.

Although the Union tries to avoid a strict conditional link between the Stability Pact and future EU membership, the project is perceived by Central and East European states precisely as such an element in the Union's eastern policies. This aspect – and the fact that it is not intended to deal with problems in Northern Ireland, the Basque country or elsewhere in Western Europe – strengthened feelings that Western Europe's approach to Central European problems is somewhat arrogant or is even intended to establish some sort of *droit de regard* on events in Central Europe. This feeling existed in countries such as Poland and the Czech Republic, which are relatively homogeneous and do not have minority problems, and was particularly strong in countries such as Romania, Slovakia, Latvia and Estonia which have large minorities on their territories. To some extent, the Pact also reinvents the wheel because some countries in Central and Eastern Europe already have negotiated bilateral agreements or are in the process of concluding one (Hungary and Romania).

The Stability Pact is still undergoing considerable change. Whereas emphasis is still placed on border and minority issues, questions of regional and functional cooperation, including problems of migration and relevant aspects of trans-European networks, are also becoming important. The whole project is moving towards furthering cooperation among the countries concerned rather than concluding only bilateral treaties between them. Although the basic concept of a three-phased process has been maintained, it is not clear what shape the Stability Pact will finally take and how it will fit into the CSCE framework or other elements of the Union's eastern policies.

The Stability Pact, NATO's PFP and WEU's intention to enhance the status of Consultation partners, all have in common the West's attempt to take more seriously the security problems in Central and Eastern Europe without giving the countries concerned what they wish for: security guarantees or full membership in Western institutions. Nevertheless, the three initiatives aim at reducing the security vacuum in Central and Eastern Europe which could lead to substantial Western involvement even if automatic commitment is to be avoided. The EU's Stability Pact and the possible enlargement of WEU's association policies also clearly signal to the countries concerned, and the outside world, that from a strategic political angle, Central Eastern Europe is no longer seen as a grey area, but one on which Western Europe has claims in terms of security and stability. The three initiatives, however, fail to address other key aspects of security related to social and economic development. Projecting stability eastwards needs to be underpinned by bolstering reform processes and encouraging economic recovery. Here, the integration policies of the EC/Union are of overriding importance.

THE ASSOCIATION POLITICS OF THE COMMUNITY

The Community has concluded so-called 'Euro-agreements' with the Visegrad countries, Bulgaria and Romania. Trade and/or cooperation agreements have been signed with the Baltic republics, Albania and Slovenia. A free trade area will be established with the Baltic states and the perspective of accession to the EU will be included in the preamble of the related new agreements. Negotiations with Russia on a partnership and cooperation agreement may soon be concluded and, because of the strategic importance of establishing special ties with Moscow, a political declaration on the bilateral relationship was already signed in Brussels on 9 December 1993. An agreement with Ukraine is also on the current agenda of the Community. Prospects for concluding negotiations with this country improved considerably when the presidents of the United States, Russia and Ukraine signed an agreement in Moscow on dismantling Ukraine's nuclear arsenals and transferring them to Russia within seven years. The (partial) ratification of START I by the Ukrainian parliament and the largely favourable parliamentary reaction to the Clinton–Yeltsin–Kravchuk deal is also a positive development, even if certain points lack clarity regarding the Lisbon Protocol.

The above-mentioned Euro-agreements with Central and East European countries are seen as a precursor to membership of the EU.[24] Flanking policies have also been developed in the framework of the European Bank for Reconstruction and Development and the PHARE programme for economic aid to Eastern Europe by 24 Western countries, which has been coordinated since its inception by the EC Commission.

Whether the new democracies can be stabilised and prepared for membership in the EU is questionable, not only because of their high unemployment and inflation rates, poverty and political uncertainties.[25] First, aid to Central and Eastern Europe is not enough, is not efficiently allocated and most is given in the form of loans and credits rather than grants. Second, the advantages and disadvantages of the Euro-agreements are unbalanced.[26] On the one hand, they offer an institutionalised political dialogue and the step-by-step creation of a free-trade area with conditions similar to the single market. The section on economic cooperation goes far beyond anything previously tackled in association agreements. On the other hand, they still provide insufficient access to EC markets, especially in those areas where the Central and East European countries have comparative advantages, such as textiles, steel and agriculture. Moreover, the Community has insisted on safeguard and anti-dumping regulations irrespective of the fact that the associate countries have to introduce hundreds of Community regulations including EC competition laws.

Even if, at the Copenhagen summit in June 1993, the EC made some minor trade concessions and committed itself to granting future membership to countries with Euro-agreements, stabilising Central and Eastern Europe will be difficult until sufficient incentives are set for the export-led growth of these countries, and for making the region more attractive to foreign investors. A timetable for the prospect of membership and the abolition (or at least drastically restricted application) of safeguard and anti-dumping rules would be of great importance. Moreover, as long as targets for a phased process of membership in the EU remain undefined, support for economic transformation and democratic development will lack effective underpinning.

The Commission, very aware of these problems, had pleaded for a significant change in association policies and in the general attitude towards pan-European unification. It not only underlined that a clear 'prospect of membership can help to bring prosperity and peace to a region where unrest still threatens to erupt as a result of poverty, nationalism and fear',[27] but also proposed more EC trade concessions, better support for private investment in Eastern Europe, and the creation of an associate or partner membership which would allow participation in certain Community policies (but without the voting rights of full members). In addition, it pleaded for the creation of a 'European political area' through special forms of participation in CFSP meetings (with an observer status), regular enlarged meetings of the Council of Ministers, or a conference of European states 'meeting at the invitation of the European Council'. These proposals referred to the idea of a European confederation, the deliberations of former Commissioner Andriessen, suggestions made in a memorandum of the Visegrad countries and recommendations of six West European foreign-policy institutes.[28]

However, the member-states were not prepared to envisage far-reaching steps towards a more upgraded partnership with Central European associates. They were unable to agree on essential trade concessions and were also reluctant to grant Central European associates any kind of observer status in relevant bodies of the EC or CFSP. Instead, they offered a more structured multilateral dialogue, but outside the framework of ordinary Union procedures. This offer came as a result of the conclusions of the June 1993 Copenhagen summit and an initiative made in December 1993 by the British and Italian Foreign Ministers, Hurd and Andreatta, for developing concrete links between the Eastern associates and the CFSP.[29] The respective decisions of the Union Council on 7 March 1994 involve: an annual 'summit' of the president of the European Council and the Commission with the heads of state and government of the associate countries; one special council on CFSP matters during each six-month presidency; meetings with the Troika; and participation in Troika démarches and joint actions under the CFSP.[30] Although Central Europeans cannot participate in meetings of the political directors or foreign ministers of the EU states, they can nominate 'shadow' political correspondents. The package will also be offered to future Central East European associates such as the Baltic states.

Agreement on this form of political dialogue was, in spite of internal differences, reached earlier than expected due to strong British insistence and the fact that the Hurd/Andreatta initiative coincided with German interests. The whole concept aims to further regionalism in political dialogue rather than to intensify bilateralism between individual countries and the EU, as many Central European countries wish. It also focuses on separate meetings on CFSP issues to preserve EU institutions. Whether, therefore, Polish ideas of partial membership in the two intergovernmental pillars of the EU (the CFSP and cooperation in home and justice affairs) have any perspective is doubtful. It would certainly facilitate a half-way eastern enlargement while full EC membership is not possible, but it would end up unravelling the Union as an entity of three closely-knit pillars which is not in the interests of most member-states.

On the whole, the cautious approach towards the eastern dimension of European integration has to do with fundamental political and economic problems. But some economic hurdles could be more easily overcome if there was consensus on the political priorities and ways of achieving them. This is lacking, however, because of diverging interests among the member-states and a lack of vision as to how an enlarged Union could work.

THE CHALLENGE OF EASTERN ENLARGEMENT
Given their different interests, the three main West European players favour three competing models of Europe. Britain prefers a widened, but not deepened Europe.[31] France, on the other hand, favours a cohesive and stronger Western Europe which may be widened to include Central and East European countries in the more distant future.[32] It fears that an eastern enlargement would further redistribute weight within the EC towards the centre of Europe. There is deeply rooted concern not only in France that enlarging the Community to include East European and EFTA countries could lead to a German-led, or at least influenced, interest block within the Union. Germany favours a wider and deeper (or at least not weaker) Europe.[33] Because of its geographical position, Germany sees itself as a bridge between Eastern and Western Europe. It hopes to realise its specific eastern interests better within a wider rather than a smaller Union, and without provoking its neighbours' suspicions. However, Germany's general approach towards eastern enlargement has become more cautious with

the experience of its own national unification which highlighted the potential problems of pan-European unification.

Beyond these differences there are other practical problems of eastern enlargement. First, achieving compatibility in economic and political structures between Western and Eastern Europe is enormously difficult. An eastern enlargement of the Community/Union is in many respects different from the previous southern enlargement because the countries of Central and Eastern Europe face the historically unprecedented task of transforming from one-party political systems with centrally planned economies to democratic pluralism and market economies.[34] Full membership of the Union will probably not be possible for another ten or 15 years, taking the Portuguese example as a precedent with its seven years of negotiations and ten years of transitory rules. Both Western and Eastern Europe must redouble their efforts to prevent a failure of the reform policies, otherwise eastern enlargement will become a pipe-dream.

The second problem is the growing political competition for Community resources. The southern Union states are not at all enthusiastic about an eastern enlargement and already today fear that financial transfers to Central and Eastern Europe could reduce the Community's resources for the internal redistribution of wealth. This situation would worsen if very poor Eastern countries became full members. Part of the dilemma will be solved by implementing the agreement increasing the Community's budget (the Delors II package) and by the accession of the relatively rich EFTA states. However, the enormous quantity of resources needed to stabilise and integrate Central and Eastern Europe can only be provided if the EU's economic prosperity is regained and secured through the step-by-step realisation of EMU.

The third problem of enlargement is linked to the political finality of European integration and its security and defence dimension. If progress can be made towards realising the objectives of the Maastricht Treaty, will security guarantees be given to new member-countries from regions bordering the former Soviet Union?

There are no clear-cut answers to this complex (and to some extent hypothetical) question. First, much will depend on the future relationship of the Union and the CIS republics, Russia in particular, and the prevention of a revival of the East–West conflict. Second, it cannot be predicted whether relatively stable and more democratic systems can be established in the European part of the CIS and whether the issue of Russian minorities can be peacefully resolved. In a pessimistic scenario, the question of security guarantees will become highly relevant to both the Central and the West Europeans. In a more optimistic scenario, defence will be less important and there would certainly be no major obstacles to establishing friendly relations between an enlarged Union and Russia. Third, uncertainties also exist over developments in Western Europe. Even with the Maastricht

Treaty now in force, whether and when a more fully fledged security and defence union can be established is an open question. Will WEU be fully absorbed by the Union, resulting in mutual defence commitments amongst the Union members? Or, at present more likely, will WEU remain separate for many years to come thus allowing a state to join the Union without necessarily becoming a full member of WEU? When, and to what extent, will NATO be enlarged to include Central and East European countries? Ideally, all members of the Union should not only be able to join WEU, but also NATO because it is the only security institution which, through its direct link with the US, can provide full security guarantees for all Union countries. That implies that an eastern enlargement of the Union would involve a corresponding widening of NATO. In view of the difficulties of achieving a consensus on such a step among all NATO allies, an enlarged Union may have to live for some time with different security zones.

The fourth problem has to do with the geographical borders of European integration. Where does Europe end?[35] Which countries – on a West–East axis – should be regarded as future members of the EU? The eastern policies of the EU imply that the countries of the Visegrad region, Bulgaria and Romania, Slovenia and the Baltic states, are potential applicants; Europe would thus end at the Western borders of the CIS. Whether all the countries in the area between the Twelve and the CIS can become members of the EU depends on their human rights records, their democratic stability and their performance as workable market economies. Romania may have problems meeting all conditions and its future relationship with Moldova may also play a role. From a strategic point of view, the full integration of the Baltic states confronts the Union with the most critical decision – even if the issue of Russian minorities in these countries could be eased, and even if Union members such as Germany (and also future Scandinavian Union states) argue strongly in favour of their accession.

The Visegrad states (and also Slovenia) are the most likely candidates to meet the conditions in the foreseeable future. But there is still some concern about Hungary's policies regarding the protection of its ethnic communities in neighbouring countries and Slovakia's stance towards its Hungarian minority. While it is hoped that the Stability Pact will help to settle these problems, Slovakia will certainly have the greatest problems meeting the economic conditions. From a security point of view, Slovakia may need to be integrated together with the three other Visegrad countries. The problem of the Hungarian minorities living in southern Slovakia could otherwise worsen if Hungary were to become a member of the Union and Slovakia not, thus widening the gap in economic development between them. Hence, in some cases, strict overall conditionality and security considerations would have to be balanced. But, in general, conditions for accession, together with a realistic perspective for membership, are the most effective lever for the Union to influence developments in Central and Eastern

Europe. Those states able to fulfil the requirements should be integrated first, in the hope that this will have a stabilising effect on the others enabling them to follow suit. This also implies changing the ideology of an 'all or no-one approach' which only increases the obstacles.

A fifth problem concerns the efficiency of West European institutions and decision-making procedures. The EU is built on the foundations of the Rome Treaty, initially designed for six members. Today managing the club of the Twelve is no easy matter; it will be even more difficult to run a Union of 16 members (after enlargement to include EFTA countries) on the basis of the same rules. But governing Europe efficiently without adapting its institutions will be impossible because of its growing heterogeneity with 20 or more members. Current weaknesses in the system would have to be overcome by strengthening institutions (the presidency, Commission, EP) and decision-making (e.g., through majority voting). The weight in voting procedures may also have to be shifted because of the increased risk of larger Community states investing in common policies – an idea which Germany and France are beginning to pursue.[36]

It is unlikely that all member-states will be prepared for radical changes in institutional rule in the near future because of the still fresh wounds of the Maastricht debates and the dispute over the blocking minority in the case of the enlargement to EFTA states. Additionally, with the perspective of greater enlargement, the gap in views on Europe's future shape will widen. Whereas for some member-states, such as Germany, an enlargement to 16, 20 or more states strengthens the case for deepening,[37] for others like Britain, it requires a looser and more intergovernmental structure.[38] As always, it will be necessary to compromise. If only slight modifications in decision-making can be agreed, an additional solution might be to make more intensive use of flexible integration methods. This would include the possibilities of opting out and being locked out (as will happen to member-states which cannot comply with the convergence criteria of EMU), in order to ensure that only those countries able to do so work together in certain policy fields. It might be worth living with some lack of cohesion in European integration if it accelerates the integration of Central and East European countries.

Conclusions
On the whole, the risks of either an eastern enlargement failing or of integration being watered down with the permanent threat of a blockade in decision-making are still high. The latter would result in nothing more than a great customs union with a powerful Germany at its centre, an unattractive option to both West and East Europeans. The first would lead to a fortress-like model of Western Europe, with attempts made to prevent the inflow of certain goods and people from the East and the 'colonising' of

eastern regions with all the consequences such a relationship brings in terms of human rights and political stability.

However, more and more Union partners recognise that a stable little Europe bordered by an arc of crisis in the east will not work. Integrating the East step by step seems to be the best cure for many of the ills in Central and Eastern Europe because of its implications for democracy and economic development. Germany is affected the most by crises in the East, and the recovery of its eastern *Länder* depends to some extent on integrating the Eastern markets into the Community. If Western Europe were unable to develop a workable strategy for eastern enlargement, Germany might feel inclined in the long run to pursue its own eastern policies which would, in turn, increase political tensions within the Union.[39] To avoid such a development, the different interests in the enlargement issue of Germany and its European partners in the West and the South must be reconciled.

Although Europe may become wider and indeed looser in view of the already relatively strong trend towards intergovernmentalism, would it not be worthwhile for Britain to reconsider its position? An enlarged, but too loose, and therefore weak, Union with its numerous members entangled in permanent rows over what to do and how to do it, will be unable to establish the necessary degree of stability in the future Europe.

The Twelve's inability to cope successfully with the Yugoslav crisis complicated relations with other countries and caused a loss of credibility in West European institutions and of confidence in an effective CFSP, notably one without any military muscle. This resulted in the greater involvement of NATO and, most of all, of the US and Russia in diplomatic efforts to find a solution to this essentially European crisis. Moreover, the fact of internal division of the EU may make other countries more interested in strengthening bilateral ties with individual West European powers. It may therefore be difficult to develop a workable CFSP as a counterweight to traditional great power diplomacy. The long-standing acceptance that there can be zones of war and peace in Europe simultaneously also did not increase Central and East European countries' sense of security. It can only be hoped that the Yugoslav crisis will either soon be resolved or remain a special (and contained) case and that other potential conflicts in Central and Eastern Europe can be prevented by applying appropriate strategies.

One such might be the European Stability Pact. But stability cannot only be achieved by aiming at preventive effects of an as yet not very precise project. The economic and social roots of conflict must also be better addressed. Thus Western security initiatives must include improved economic offers, notably wider access to West European markets, and measures for supporting the democratic forces in Central Europe by offering participation in West European structures.

Because of the huge economic problems of widening the EC/EU towards the east, there is a tendency to advance more rapidly in the security fields.

However, this also has its limits and, in the near future, a true enlargement of either NATO or WEU will face great difficulties. It could overstretch their functions, and dilute cohesion and defence commitments (which would be in the interests of neither existing nor potential members). Progress towards the eastwards extension of the Western stability zone has to be made in line with all relevant institutions. Thus there is a need not only for parallels between WEU's bold plan for an enhanced relationship with Central East European countries and the EC/Union's association policies, but also for a full equivalent on the part of NATO. The same applies in the longer term. Once the Union is widened to the East, membership of both Alliances should be possible. But a concrete decision on this cannot be one of purely institutional logic. A variety of conditions will have to be met and such a decision has to be taken in the context of developments in the security environment.

CONCLUSIONS

The changes which have taken place in the international security environment, as well as within the EC/EU, since the end of East–West antagonism are much more profound than was expected when the Maastricht Treaty was negotiated in 1991. It is now difficult to imagine that a fully fledged EU could be developed in the foreseeable future. Moreover, the Maastricht Treaty has complicated many things: the acceptance of supra-national integration has been weakened; the institutional dilemmas of Western security policy have been increased; and the enlargement of the EU has become more difficult, *inter alia*, because of the defence dimension of the Union Treaty. But the non-Maastricht case would be even worse. Who would be able to provide the necessary structures and mechanisms to overcome the division of Europe, if not the European Union? What would be Europe's future without any commitments to objectives for political and security integration?

However, the Maastricht Treaty, negotiated on the basis of a traditional West European model of integration, needs to be revised in order to contribute much better to the development of a new security order in the wider Europe. Avoiding the necessary decisions by moving forward incrementally, with one step here and one step there on various institutional levels, in the hope that this will lead by itself to a qualitative leap is not enough. The result is that overlaps in the membership and functions of individual institutions create a considerable degree of confusion, causing inefficiency and duplication of work. What is necessary is to reduce organisational complexity and to develop a clearer and more realistic division of labour between the relevant institutions involved in European and international security.

Today Europe does not represent a power able to cope successfully with conflicts and crises which have a military dimension, as shown in the Yugoslav crisis. What is lacking is the common political will and the necessary military capacities to give it the stature and credibility of a serious security actor. Europe is still far away from a common defence policy and a common defence and what has up to now been developed in WEU operationally can be described as first steps in that direction. The development of an identity of security interests, a basic precondition for taking collective action, is obviously also a long-term process. It can only succeed if the governments concerned learn that Europe is an entity, whether individual interests always coincide or not. As long as Europe as such does not have enough military muscle, its contribution to the management of acute crises will remain very limited or at least confined to coordinating diplomatic efforts. This does not mean that Europe needs a large intervention force, but it does need sufficient military capability which could underpin its crisis diplomacy, and which could be used collectively for operations such as humanitarian missions and peacekeeping.

The strength of West European institutions lies in their capacity to shape the political and economic order on a nearby continental scale through their association and enlargement strategies. Including other European states in the system created by the West Europeans over four decades is the prime task of integration policies in order to structure relations among a greater number of European nations in a peaceful way. However, an enlargement to include the EFTA states could still fail, and when Central and East European countries can join the EU is an open question. A true, new European order will only come about if widening the EU to 16, 20 or more states succeeds. That is the greatest challenge facing the EU, and internal differences over the issue, as well as economic problems – protectionism in Western Europe, economic transformation in Central and Eastern Europe – represent great obstacles. Apart from that, however, there exists a fundamental dilemma: in order to serve the purpose of stability on the continent, a federal construction of Europe would be necessary. But as more states enter the Union, the more difficult it will be to deepen integration between all members. Hence, there is the real risk that enlargement will lead to disintegration as compared to what has been achieved among the 12 EU states. Should Europe transform into something like a great free-trade area with only loose political ties among the states concerned, the gains in stability will be small. A political structure to steer the processes on the continent and to balance developments in the former Soviet Union would then be missing. Germany, whether it liked it or not, would be the strongest nation in the middle of the continent, with quasi-satellite relations with neighbouring states, notably in the East, thus reanimating old problems of the balance of power in Europe. The member-states need to realise that there is no alternative to deepening before or in parallel with widening in order to ensure the efficiency and stability of a bigger Union. Even if the vision of a wider and homogeneously deeper Union has to be abandoned, a core group made up of present West European member-states needs to proceed with integration in order to be able to manage the whole enterprise and to secure a workable peace system.

European integration *à la* Maastricht has without doubt complicated US–European relations at a time when it was (and still is) difficult to adapt them to the new post-Cold War situation. On the other hand, the security and defence mechanisms created by the Maastricht Treaty increased the possibilities of a more balanced transatlantic relationship and of transforming the Alliance into a two-pillar structure – better suited to the different geopolitical interests after the Cold War. Had the CFSP not been initiated three years ago and WEU not developed operationally, West Europeans would have to do so today, and under much less favourable circumstances, in order to compensate for the partial retreat of the US and America's growing reluctance to become involved with forces in the management of 'minor' conflicts. On the whole, the Maastricht developments are positive for transatlantic relations, not least since the US itself has articulated its clear interest in a more assertive Europe as a security partner. The problem is that the EU and WEU are still too weak to fulfil that role. Europe's present relations with America can be described as dependence with growing uncertainties because of the US tendency to approach European security problems selectively. This also finds its expression in a greater complexity of European and Atlantic military structures and doubts about whether concepts like Combined Joint Task Forces will be implemented successfully and work in practice. The situation can only be improved if the Europeans are truly prepared to take over responsibility when the Americans hesitate to act or do not wish to become directly involved. Europeans need, therefore, to clarify their concept of security. They have to consider whether they prefer an isolationist or an interventionist policy and when, and under what conditions, they deem it necessary to become militarily engaged. Keeping options open for the latter requires Europe to develop appropriate capabilities and a common strategic vision on crisis management in order to be able to contribute more effectively to collective security.

Even if at present collective defence is not the prime concern of the West, the situation will change with the enlargement of the EU to the borders of Russia and other CIS countries. Hence, the issue of a common defence policy of the EU and, most of all, a common defence, will become essential and will involve all the problems associated with the future Euro-Atlantic security architecture. That could already start with an inclusion of EFTA states into the EU, even if countries such as Finland do not yet wish to join fully either WEU or NATO. Their attitude may change in time, however, and once Poland or the Baltic states enter the Union the problem will become even more acute. There are no grounds for alarm and much will depend on the development of the strategic environment, but sooner or later a decision has to be made on who will guarantee the security of new members in the Eastern parts of the Union – WEU, NATO or the Union itself? If the EU/WEU states are not prepared to bear the consequences in terms of costs and risks or if no alternative security arrangement can be found with the US, the Union as a whole cannot become a defence community.

Renationalisation versus integration
The end of the Cold War has not made it any easier to develop a common foreign, security and defence policy, nor to overcome hurdles of national sovereignty on the way towards a more integrated Europe. With no common threat, differences in risk and threat perceptions have grown, underlining the problem of fragmenting security interests. In addition, domestic factors have become highly relevant. Parliaments and public opinion exert

increasing influence on governments, and the development of national interests does not favour greater European unity. Britain still remains insular, France still has problems with its Gaullist heritage and Germany has become a more 'normal' country – not only following the judgment of the Bundesverfassungsgericht on the Maastricht Treaty, but also in view of its search for a national identity since unification. What will be the future of a common security and defence policy if Germany remains unable to contribute militarily to crisis management and if Britain and France show no interest in a European nuclear strategy? The internal division of the EU in the case of the former Yugoslavia has only weakened the prospects of a common security policy and strengthened moves towards great-power diplomacy. The arrival of the UN as an important actor in European security has furthered this trend. Other centrifugal forces, spin-offs of the enlargement policies of the Union and WEU, also make it more difficult to achieve security and defence integration.

Europeans need to decide whether they wish to rely on unpredictable *ad hoc* coalitions of principal nations, or on a more integrated common security policy. The chances for continued integration on the basis of the Maastricht Treaty and its revision in 1996 are not too bad because of the limited capabilities of the nation-state, first, to respond independently to a variety of security challenges (even if they do not directly affect the security of the country in question), and, second, to cope autonomously with long-term economic problems, particularly strong economic competition from the US and Japan. Third, the insistence on national sovereignty is a defensive strategy. In a world of interdependence and a closely economically and politically intertwined Europe, the unavoidable erosion of national autonomy can only be compensated by participation in collective decision-making. In addition, all Union member-states are redefining their security policies and seeking ways in which best to deal with both their individual and their shared concerns. Integrating other countries into the framework of the EU is a further challenge which provides incentives for cooperation rather than isolation. Finally, and paradoxically, the new role of the UN in European and worldwide security also has a positive impact on the future development of the Union and its security dimension. The UN of today is confronted with overstretched financial and military capacities and will have increasingly to rely on the support of regional organisations to develop a system of universal security. But that also requires better coordination between European security institutions and the UN, and an understanding on the part of the member-states of the importance of acting more collectively.

The question of a new dynamic in European integration will depend greatly on the development of the Franco-German relationship, which has been weakened by the monetary crisis, divergencies over the handling of the Yugoslav conflict, differences over free trade, and the need and speed with which fully to integrate Central and Eastern Europe. These problems notwithstanding, France and Germany have continued strategic interests in European integration, and the development of a closer Union and a more effective CFSP can come about if the two countries are able to develop joint views and initiatives. These have to be presented to partner countries in a diplomatic way in order to avoid counterproductive results and to facilitate the participation of other members, notably Britain which holds the key to many questions of Europe's future.

The CFSP and international security

What contributions to international and European security can be expected in the near future by the CFSP and joint actions in that framework? A dynamic policy is likely towards CSCE matters, arms control and confidence-building in Europe, export-control policies and nuclear non-proliferation (notably with a view to the 1995 NPT review conference), even if much more substance must be added to common policies in these fields. Other joint activities are already on the agenda, such as the European Stability Pact, and political and economic support for the peace efforts in the Near East and South Africa.

To avoid Western Europe being surrounded by an arc of crisis from the Baltics to the Balkans and the Black Sea to the Mediterranean, the Union's CFSP and joint actions will have to focus in the next two years on Central Europe, Russia, Ukraine, the former Yugoslavia and the Mediterranean (especially the Maghreb). Western Europe's deeper involvement in Central Europe will be unavoidable to secure stability, support democratic and economic development, avoid negative spill-overs to the West from political maldevelopment or potential crises, and strengthen the likelihood of EC associates becoming members of the EU. This will involve direct engagement through mediation or arbitration where necessary and regular intensified political dialogue and consultation, including joint foreign-policy actions between the EU and Central European associates. Some sort of strategic partnership needs to be developed with Russia, not in order to compete with the US, but in order to prevent Russia from feeling isolated by the expansive logic of European integration. Ukraine cannot be left out of Eastern policies either and joint action may become necessary to prevent the country from falling apart. As for the former Yugoslavia, efforts to find a solution to the crisis as soon as possible have to be strengthened through the organisation of coordinated international pressure on all conflicting parties. The 'hour' of Europe will come in the period following a political settlement. To help to reconstruct Bosnia and other Yugoslav successor states, to initiate an arms-control regime for the Balkans and to offer, at some stage, appropriate forms of participation in European integration – all these would be essential elements of an EU post-conflict strategy. As for the Mediterranean and the Maghreb, EU joint action will have to concentrate on establishing a workable political dialogue, accompanied by appropriate measures to help overcome the acute socio-economic problems which are creating migration or refugee flows. Paying greater attention to Mediterranean issues is necessary to reassure the southern EU states that their interests will not be brushed aside when coping with the eastern dimension of integration.

On the whole, the contribution of the Union and its CFSP to European and international security will be more diplomatic, political and economic than military. However, political and economic instruments for crisis management need to be improved. They are not useless, but they have little or no effect once a conflict has escalated militarily. Therefore, it will be necessary to develop a variety of preventive strategies. Preparing them in advance could reduce problems of consensus, which are difficult to overcome in times of stress. This also implies the creation of sufficient capacities for a common risk analysis and for a common planning of preventive action within the CFSP section of the Union's secretariat and within the Commission in order to design a cohesive and early approach to a potential conflict.

The primarily civil character of the Union's strategic assets does not exclude it from playing an active role in the management of acute crises. The Union can support UN and CSCE activities by financial means, food aid or personnel from member-states and it can call upon member-states or request WEU to prepare military contributions to UN operations and peacekeeping activities. Finally, as many conflicts and tensions are rooted in political, social and economic instabilities, the Union is much better equipped than any other international organisation to address related problems.

Looking ahead to 1996, what should be done to overcome at least parts of the weaknesses of the present CFSP system? Some more common structures of the CFSP in Brussels need to be established since member- states tend to *re*-act rather than to *pre*-act. The Commission should be allowed to assume the role of a true thirteenth player in the CFSP in order better to represent a supranational counterweight to purely national interests. Procedures need to be developed to reflect more adequately the weight of the EU in international affairs, even in cases where there is not full consensus among foreign ministers. It may also be appropriate to reconsider the principle of half-annually rotating presidencies in as far as the foreign-policy representation of the EU is concerned. Most of all, a security concept needs to be developed, aiming at options for a variety of flexible joint policy responses to violations of international peace. It can only be based on generally identified common security interests and mechanisms for defining particular ones in a given crisis. As regards the aim of introducing a common defence policy, it will be necessary to define the possible scope of such a policy and to clarify what kind of commitments member-states would be required to make if they coordinated aspects of their military security policies.

The military dimension of European integration
Whether and when the Union can be transformed into a more fully fledged entity with a common defence is an open question. Much will depend on the future strategic situation, NATO's further performance and the development of European integration itself. The maximum conceivable at present is the integration of WEU into the EU over a longer period, perhaps starting in 1998 or 1999. But whether agreement on this can be reached in 1996 is unclear. Many member-states prefer a cautious approach to political integration and wish to postpone steps towards defence integration until some time in the future. Western Europe is thus still a long way from having an integrated army and a common nuclear deterrent. However, what is clearly discernible is a trend towards pooling sovereignty in areas of military security, even if that is not yet far enough advanced. WEU can still be described as an organisation in its operational development. Its contribution to crisis management up to now has been rather limited, the value of its Article V guarantee has much to do with the fact that most of its members participate in NATO's military integration. On the other hand, it is precisely the latter fact which gives WEU greater flexibility in its eastern policies so that it can include Central Europeans in its own structures and give them the possibility of attending Council meetings. WEU can thus make an important contribution to projecting stability eastwards through an intensified and regular security dialogue and through bringing Central European countries closer to the EU and, to some extent also, to NATO.

Many politicians and experts in NATO/WEU countries have repeatedly criticised WEU for a perceived tendency to produce redundant security structures and to weaken NATO's activities. While there was a period of rivalry between the two institutions (notably between spring and autumn 1992), this view can no longer be upheld. So far WEU has been more overshadowed by NATO than the other way round, and the problems which NATO still has are more related to the situation in the post-Cold War era than to the existence of WEU. Second, WEU has established close working relations with NATO and, since the January 1994 Alliance summit, the possibilities of practical military cooperation between them have significantly improved. Third, as fundamental changes are underway in transatlantic relations, Europeans need an appropriate forum to coordinate their policies on Alliance affairs and on dealing with non-Article V missions. Thus cooperation in WEU has more to do with an enlarged Alliance diplomacy than with a policy aimed at rivalling NATO and US interests. Will, however, the Europeans be ready and able to act where necessary? This would require a consensus among them on how to react, as well as the consent of the US if Europeans needed to use NATO headquarters, command structures and communication lines.

If the member-states wish WEU to become a better-prepared organisation for dealing with non-Article V missions they need to develop its capacities further, including logistics, transportation, communications and satellite intelligence. The troops who would in fact be available for peace-keeping have to be more precisely defined and the appropriate training ensured. The organisational structures of WEU may need some improvement in order to make it possible for non-Article V missions to be carried out independently, and this could also be important if NATO assets are used. Without such further steps, WEU would have enormous difficulties contributing significantly to collective security or backing the crisis diplomacy of the European Union. As regards 1996, it is necessary to clarify what a common defence policy means in the post-Cold War era. Elements of such a policy must be defined by WEU and their implications considered in terms of costs, practicability and compatibility with NATO.

Rethinking integration: widening and deepening

This paper argues that the deepening versus widening debate is fruitless as long as it assumes that integration can proceed in exactly the same way as it has done for most of the last four decades. A more flexible concept will be required to deepen and widen European integration, to solve the related institutional problems and to satisfy the different interests of the present member-states. The only realistic solution is to move forward at different speeds, with different tiers of membership in certain policy areas, but within a single institutional framework. This could reduce institutional redundancy and help to overcome present or future members' unwillingness or inability to participate fully in more integrated policy areas. It would imply possibilities for opting out as well as being locked out from certain policy fields on the basis of strict criteria. Further deepening in 1996 will also require the reduction of the democratic deficit of integration (e.g., through the creation of a second parliamentary chamber) and the strengthening of precisely defined responsibilities of the Presidency, the Commission and the EP. Qualified majority voting, in combination with changed voting weights for larger member-countries, will increasingly have to be used in EC matters and introduced into CFSP affairs. Otherwise, consensus problems will grow in an enlarged Union, without any chance of overcoming a lack of leadership. The art of integration will be, on the one hand, to use more flexible methods without turning the concept of European integration into an *à la carte* model and, on the other hand, to strengthen the possibilities of 'selective deepening' in order to enhance the capacities for managing the whole enterprise. In the longer term, Europe might be organised around two overlapping circles: one made up of countries which can proceed with monetary integration; the other made up of those countries which can go ahead with a common defence policy. Both groups of EU countries would centre around the Franco-German relationship which would have to continue to serve as a motor for integration.

It is true that the integration of Central and Eastern Europe faces enormous structural difficulties and that full membership of the countries concerned in the EU is not a realistic option in the foreseeable future. However, economic and societarian incompatibility should not prevent them from being offered some sort of direct participation in integration policies. Granting partial membership to Central and East Europeans by opening up the intergovernmental pillars of the Union for full participation in CFSP or home and justice affairs is not a solution. It would cause the Union to unravel as an entity and would only further institutional proliferation with all its negative effects. Instead, Central and East European countries should be given observer status in certain EC and CFSP policy areas. This would better acquaint them with the social fabric of integration and make them feel they truly belong to Europe. Together with the opening of EC markets, it might be the most useful step in preventing serious backlashes throughout the difficult period of transition. Full admittance to the Union can only be conditional on the accomplishment of certain economic norms and political rules of behaviour, including respecting borders and guaranteeing minority rights. But step-by-step integration is what makes the prospect of membership more realistic, thus strengthening the most important lever which Western Europe possesses to influence developments in Central and Eastern Europe.

The security of an enlarged Union
It is obviously not possible to achieve a formal eastern expansion of the alliances (NATO and WEU) more easily and earlier than an enlargement of the EU towards the east. The strengthening of cooperation with Central and East Europeans through PFP and WEU's intention to enhance its relationship with countries which have, or soon will have, Euro-agreements are certainly steps in the right direction – even if they fall short of offering full membership or security guarantees. The longer-term perspectives need, however, more careful consideration. With the enlargement of the Union to EFTA countries and, in future, to Central and East European states, Western Europe will lose the special zone separating it from the former Soviet Union. Moreover, it may lead to a non-homogeneous security area within the EU. Throughout the Cold War, the question of security guarantees and membership in West European institutions posed no problems because virtually the whole EC area was covered by NATO. In a widened Union, the only way to create a unique strategic area would be either to enlarge NATO (and simultaneously WEU) to include new members of the Union, or significantly to build up WEU's defence structures and capabilities, including a credible deterrent, to guarantee the security of all Union mem-

bers. The first option is the most clear-cut, and would not cause WEU any difficulties in maintaining its role as the European pillar of the Alliance (the same would apply to the EU should it absorb WEU). However, it would make enlargement of the Union dependent on American readiness to extend formal security guarantees to other areas in Europe, and on the willingness of all EU countries, including France, to accept such an all-embracing role for NATO. There is also the problem of whether an enlargement of NATO would suit the strategic situation of post-Cold War Europe and whether it would affect the cohesion of the Alliance.

The second option, a major build-up of WEU, is unrealistic in the foreseeable future – given the financial consequences alone – even if it eliminated the problem of developing a European defence policy based on security guarantees given by a non-Union member, the US. This would imply creating a fully fledged defence organisation to exist in parallel with NATO, which would certainly meet with strong resistance from many countries which are against the undermining, and finally dissolution, of NATO. As long as the Atlantic Alliance is not extended to the north and the east, and a European defence community is not in sight, an enlarged Union will therefore have to live with different security zones.

This might have a positive effect in the sense of avoiding the revival of any bloc confrontation in Europe. On the other hand, it might also prove to be a fair-weather model which could quickly come under pressure if a new, peripheral Union member-state were subjected to a serious external threat or even an attack. But, in such a case, notably if the overall strategic balance were threatened, WEU, NATO and the US could not simply stand back. It could therefore be argued that some sort of existential security guarantee existed (not an automatic or treaty-bound one). However, all that would not be the best in the longer term for the internal cohesion of the Union because of unfavourable psychological effects and possible conflicts of interest over security issues and related policy-making. A lasting solution would require NATO's enlargement or a European defence which would at least be able to protect the eastern borders of a widened Union long before any massive Western reaction became necessary.

Worst-case scenarios and potential external threats to future Union members apart, many sources of instability in Central and Eastern Europe are non-military, although they could escalate into armed conflict. The traditional instruments of Western security institutions (including formal security guarantees) are relatively useless for dealing with domestic instability and ethnic conflicts. The step-by-step integration of these countries into West European structures with their political and economic advantages and well-tried institutional mechanisms for internal conflict management, together with other elements of multilateral cooperation, seems more appropriate. Finally, anything which could create new divisions in Europe should be avoided. This means not making eastern enlargement of the Union dependent on strict defence considerations – and thus limiting widening to only a few countries – or by drawing new bloc lines with respect to the former Soviet Union, notably Russia.

The East–West and West–West dimensions
One of the key issues for stability in Europe and for an enlargement of the EU concerns developments in the former Soviet Union and future relations between it and West European institutions. In Russia, the power struggle has not been resolved and the prospects for democratic development and economic reforms are bleak. Moreover, it is in the process of reorganising its 'near-abroad' and the idea of building a greater Russia has the widespread support of the strengthened 'red-brown' political forces and the military. If Russia 'returned' to an aggressive foreign policy, defence considerations would again be high on the Western agenda. Everything should be done to create a favourable international environment to support moderate forces in Russia and increase the costs of an anti-Western foreign policy. That also implies establishing a well-founded cooperative relationship with Russia on the part of both the EU and WEU, in order to prevent negative Russian reactions to Western Europe's enlargement policies. Russia must be assured that there is no intention to isolate it, that it is not excluded from the construction of Europe and that it can benefit from widened integration. It will also be important to pay greater political attention to Ukraine, which has so far been over-shadowed by the West's preoccupation with Russia. A basic interest of a widened EU will be to have Ukraine as an independent and non-nuclear neighbour.

The most important relationship for Western Europe is that with the United States. Adapting it to the new conditions of the post-Cold War era remains high on the policy agenda. The transatlantic ideological quarrels of the past over a European defence identity have been settled and the chances for developing a renewed partnership are better than a few years ago. However, substantial problems in European–US relations now play a greater role, notably where security interests do not coincide. Economic conflicts and the Union's eastern policies will also cause greater problems. Moreover, Europe may be entangled for years with its integration problems and the US preoccupied with domestic affairs. Neither presents the best preconditions for managing the transatlantic security community in an era of strategic change.

NATO alone will be unable to cope with the broad range of issues affecting future transatlantic relations. This paper therefore argues for more formalised links between the EU and the US administration. The mechanisms which have been created with the transatlantic declaration of 1990 need to be strengthened or, maybe more appropriately, a new Atlantic Charter should be negotiated between the EU and the US to cover security and other relevant issues. This should logically include better procedures and mechanisms for regulating economic conflicts in order to prevent costly trade wars and to manage – together with Japan (a rather neglected dimension of European policy) – global interdependence. Most of all, Western Europe needs to talk to the US at some stage about the security implications of its enlargement policies since a new European security order cannot be constructed without a close and reliable transatlantic partnership. The problem is that the US administration seems not to be fully aware of the importance of the issue and European governments tend to ignore the problems involved. However, harmonising the enlargement policies of the EU and NATO will become the most critical question in future European–US relations, thus marking the real watershed in the development of Atlantic and European defence structures. Much is at stake: the long-term prospects of the transatlantic security link and the remaking of Europe through expanded integration.

Notes

Chapter I

[1] See Pierre Gerbet, *La construction de l'Europe* (Paris: Imprimerie nationale, 1983); Lothar Brock and Mathias Jopp (eds), *Sicherheitspolitische Zusammenarbeit und Kooperation der Rüstungswirtschaft in Westeuropa* (Baden-Baden: NOMOS, 1986).

[2] For the relevant EPC documents, see *EPZ-Dokumentation* (Bonn: Auswärtiges Amt, 1987).

[3] See Rome Declaration of 27 October 1984, reprinted in *The Reactivation of WEU. Statements and Communiqués 1984–1987* (London: Secretariat-General of Western European Union, 1988), pp. 5–15.

[4] One such case was the formulation of the WEU Platform on European Security Interests on 27 October 1987 during the INF debate which underlined the interest of WEU member-states in maintaining strategic coupling with the US despite nuclear disarmament. The document is reprinted in *The Reactivation of WEU*, pp. 37–45.

[5] See William Wallace (ed.), *The Dynamics of European Integration* (London and New York: Pinter, 1990).

[6] For the analysis of events, see Mathias Jopp and Wolfgang Wessels, 'Institutional Frameworks for Security Cooperation in Western Europe: Development and Options', in Mathias Jopp, Reinhardt Rummel and Peter Schmidt (eds), *Integration and Security in Western Europe* (Boulder, CO; San Francisco, CA; and Oxford: Westview, 1991), pp. 35–73. For the text of the Mitterrand–Kohl initiative, see *Agence Europe*, no. 5238, 20 April 1990. See also the European Council, Dublin, 25–26 June 1990, 'Presidency Conclusions', *Europe Documents,* nos. 1632–33, 29 June 1990.

[7] See, for example, the far-reaching proposals of the European Commission before and during the IGC on political union, reprinted in *Europe Documents*, no. 1659, 31 October 1990, and nos. 1697–98, 7 March 1991. See also Jacques Delors, 'European Integration and Security', *Survival*, vol. 33, no. 2, March–April 1991, pp. 99–109.

[8] For an example of American interests, see the speech by the US Ambassador to NATO, William Taft, at the IISS, London, 11 February 1991, reported in *Agence Europe, no.* 5429, 11–12 February 1991. For other examples, see Edward Mortimer, *European Security after the Cold War*, Adelphi Paper 271 (London: Brassey's for the IISS, 1992), Chapter IV.

[9] See Anand Menon, Anthony Forster and William Wallace, 'A Common European Defence?', *Survival*, vol. 34, no. 3, Autumn 1992, pp. 98–118, and Trevor Taylor, 'The Future of West European Security and Defence Cooperation: United Kingdom Positions', paper presented at a conference of the Stiftung Wissenschaft und Politik, Ebenhausen, 10–11 April 1991.

[10] For Denmark's interests, see its memoranda presented before and during the IGC on political union, *Agence Europe,* no. 5353, 19 October 1990, pp. 5–6; no. 5456, 29 March 1991, pp. 5–6; and no. 5465, 5 April 1991, p. 4.

[11] For the February and October 1991 CFSP proposals of France and Germany in the framework of the

IGC on political union, see *Europe Documents*, no. 1690, 15 February 1991 and *Europe Documents*, no. 1738, 18 October 1991.

[12] As evidence, see the Franco-German–Spanish joint communiqué on political union, 11 October 1991, in *Europe Documents,* no. 1737, 17 October 1991.

[13] For Greek interests in political union, see P. Nikiforos Diamandouros and Athanassios G. Platias, in Jopp, Rummel and Schmidt (eds), *Integration and Security in Western Europe*, pp. 215–29.

[14] Italy already proposed this in summer 1990 and again at an early stage of the IGC on political union. See *Agence Europe,* no. 5331, 19 September 1990, p. 3, and *Atlantic News,* no. 2296, 8 February 1991, p. 3.

[15] See David Yost, 'France and West European Defence Identity', *Survival*, vol. 33, no. 4, July–August 1991, pp. 327–51; Nicole Gnesotto, *European Defence: Why Not the Twelve?*, Chaillot Paper 1 (Paris: WEU Institute for Security Studies, 1991); Ian Gambles, *European Security Integration in the 1990s*, Chaillot Paper 3, November 1991.

[16] See, among others, Dominique Moïsi, 'The French Answer to the German Question', *European Affairs*, vol. 4, no. 1, 1990, pp. 30–35.

[17] See Elizabeth Pond, 'Germany in the New Europe', *Foreign Affairs*, vol. 71, no. 2, Spring 1992, pp. 114–30.

[18] See Peter Schmidt, *The Special Franco-German Security Relationship in the 1990s*, Chaillot Paper 8 (Paris: WEU Institiute for Security Studies, June 1993), p. 44.

[19] See the Luxembourg draft treaty of 18 June 1991, *Europe Documents*, nos. 1722–23, 5 July 1991.

[20] The Dutch draft treaty was summarised in *Agence Europe*, no. 5564, 11 September 1991, pp. 3–4.

[21] For the Kohl-Mitterrand proposals on foreign policy, security and defence, see *Europe Documents*, no. 1738, 18 October 1991.

[22] See also Menon, Forster and Wallace, 'A Common European Defence?'

[23] See the Rome Declaration on Peace and Cooperation, issued by the 16 heads of state and government, Rome, 7–8 November 1991 (Brussels: NATO Information and Press Office, 1991), para. 6.

[24] See the Treaty on European Union, (Luxembourg: Office for Official Publications of the European Communities, 1992).

[25] For an assessment, see Otto Schmuck, 'Der Maastrichter Vertrag zur europäische Union. Fortschritt und Ausdifferenzierung der europäischen Einigung', *Europa-Archiv*, no. 4, 1992, pp. 97–106.

[26] See Wolfgang Wessels, 'Maastricht: Ergebnisse, Bewertungen und Langzeittrends', *Integration*, no. 1, 1992, pp. 2–16.

[27] For the Commission's engagement in the debate on security issues, see the study of seven West European institutes which was stimulated and supported by the Commission *Confronting Insecurity in Eastern Europe: Challenges for the European Community* (English language edition: London, Chatham House, December 1992)

[28] See the Resolution of the European Parliament on the Perspectives of a European Security Policy, 10 June 1991, EP Doc. AS3-107/91 (PE 152.801).

[29] On the role of the EP in external

relations, see Wolfgang Wessels, 'The EC and the New European Architecture – the European Union as a Trustee for a (pan)-European Wheel', speech given at the Institut d'Etudes européennes, Brussels, 7 February 1992, pp. 13 and 14.

[30] See the Treaty on European Union (English version), p. 239.

[31] See Elfriede Regelsberger, 'Die Gemeinsame Aussen – und Sicherheitspolitik nach Maastricht – Minimalreformen in neuer Entwicklungsperspektive', *Integration*, no. 2, 1992, pp. 83–93.

[32] See Willem F. van Eekelen, 'The Changing Environment of Transatlantic Relations', European Strategic Group, ESG-Report, Paris, 1991.

Chapter II

[1] See the detailed analysis of Otto Schmuck, 'Heterogene Diskussionslandschaft zu Maastricht: Die Ratifizierungsdebatte zum Vertrag über die Europäische Union', *Integration*, no. 4, 1992, pp. 206–15.

[2] For the debate in the Netherlands, see Bob van den Bos, *Can Atlanticism Survive? The Netherlands and the New Role of Security Institutions* (Clingendael, The Hague: The Netherlands Institute of International Relations, July 1992).

[3] See Schmuck, 'Heterogene Diskussionslandschaft', pp. 210–11.

[4] See Conclusions of the Presidency, European Council of Edinburgh, 11–12 December 1992, *Agence Europe* (special edition), no. 5878, 13 December 1992, pp. 9–11.

[5] The judgment of the Bundesverfassungsgericht, 12 October 1993, is reprinted in *Europa-Archiv*, no. 22, 1993, pp. D460–D476.

[6] See Heidemarie Wieczorek-Zeul, 'Der Vertrag von Maastricht im Deutschen Bundestag', *Europa-Archiv*, nos 13–14, 1993, pp. 405–12.

[7] The first report, 'The Likely Development of the CFSP', was published in *Agence Europe*, no. 5761, 29–30 June 1992, Annex; for an abstract of the second report, 'Joint Action and the Development of the Common Foreign and Security Policy in the Field of Security', see *Agence Europe*, nos 5874–75, 9–10 December 1992; for an abstract of the third report on the 'Analysis of European Security Interests in the New Strategic Context . . . ', see *Agence Europe*, no. 5995, 7–8 June 1993.

[8] See Conclusions of the Presidency, European Council of Copenhagen, 21–22 June 1993, para. 10, *Europe Documents*, nos 1844–45, 24 June 1993, pp. 1–16.

[9] See the European Commission's report , 'The Challenge of Enlargement', *Europe Documents*, no. 1790, 3 July 1992, paras 16 and 17.

[10] See Reinhard Meier-Walser, 'Germany, France and Britain on the Threshold of a New Europe', *Aussenpolitik*, no. 4, 1992, pp. 334–42.

[11] See Wolfgang Wessels, 'Erweiterung, Vertiefung, Verkleinerung', *Europa-Archiv*, no. 10, 1993, pp. 308–16.

[12] This became clear during the Franco-German Summit on 4 December 1992 in Bonn.

[13] See Krister Wahlbäck, 'Der unwägbare Osten. Eine schwedische Sicht neuer Sicherheitsprobleme', *Europa-Archiv*, no. 3, 1993, pp. 59–64; Paul Luif, 'L'élargissement aux pays de l'AELE', *Politique étrangère*, no. 1, 1993, pp. 63–77; and the address of the Finnish Defence Minister, Elizabeth Rehn, to the WEU Assembly at its 39th

Ordinary Session (First Part), *Official Report of Debates* (Paris: Assembly of Western European Union, June 1993), pp. 168–70.

[14] See Elfriede Regelsberger, 'Neutral EFTA Countries on the Doorstep of European Union', paper prepared for the WEU Institute for Security Studies, Paris, September 1992.

[15] This became evident in WEU seminars with participants from neutral EFTA governments; see also Ernst Sucharipa, 'Von der Neutralität zur europäischen Sicherheitsidentität: Österreich und die Europäische Union', *Integration*, no. 3, 1993, pp. 158–62.

[16] See 'Finnland denkt nicht an NATO-Beitritt', *Frankfurter Allgemeine Zeitung*, 2 February 1994.

[17] See Willem Van Eekelen, 'Western European Union in the Emerging European Security Architecture', *Canadian Defence Quarterly*, vol. 21, no 4, 1992, February 1992; Eekelen, 'WEU's post-Maastricht Agenda,' *NATO Review*, vol. 40, no. 2, April 1992, pp. 13–17.

[18] Among the intergovernmental bodies of WEU below the level of the Permanent Council, the most important are the Council Working Group, the Special Working Group, (made up primarily of representatives of foreign ministries) and the Defence Representatives Group. There is also a Mediterranean Working Group, two expert groups on verification in connection with the Open Skies and the CFE Treaties and *ad hoc* groups on space and on the former Yugoslavia.

[19] See the declaration on the role of WEU and its relations with the EU and the Atlantic Alliance, adopted by the nine WEU member-states on 10 December 1991 in Maastricht.

[20] See also Lopez Henares report, 'European Armaments Cooperation after Maastricht', *WEU Assembly Document*, no. 1332, 23 October 1992.

[21] See the Petersberg Declaration of the WEU Ministerial Council, 19 June 1992, Part II, *Europe Documents*, no. 1787, 23 June 1992.

[22] See the declaration of the WEU Council of Ministers, Luxembourg, 22 November 1993, Part I, para. 4.

[23] Petersberg Declaration, Part II, para. 4.

[24] See the WEU Council's communiqué, Rome, 20 November 1992.

[25] See 'Declaration on WEU Observers', drawn up by the WEU Council of Ministers, Rome, 20 November 1992.

[26] See the document on associate membership of WEU of Iceland, Norway and Turkey, reprinted in *WEU Assembly Document*, no. 1351, 25 November 1992.

[27] See the final communiqué of the Ministerial meeting of the North Atlantic Council (NAC), Oslo, 4 June 1992, *NATO Press Communiqué*, M-NAC-1 (92) 59, paras 11 and 13; the communiqué of the NAC meeting, Brussels, 17 December 1992, is reprinted in *Atlantic News*, no. 2484, 1992.

[28] See William Walker and Philip Gummet, *Nationalism, Internationalism and the European Defence Market*, Chaillot Paper 9 (Paris: WEU Institute for Security Studies, September 1993).

[29] See the declaration of the WEU Council of Ministers, Luxembourg, 22 November 1993, para. 3.

[30] See the declaration of the heads of state and government at the NAC meeting, Brussels, 10–11 January 1994, *Atlantic Document*, no. 83, 12 January 1994, paras 6 and 9.

See François Heisbourg, 'The European–US Alliance: Valedictory Reflections on Continental Drift in the post-Cold War Era', *International Affairs*, vol. 68, no. 4, 1992, pp. 665–78, and the address of NATO's Secretary-General, Manfred Wörner, to the WEU Assembly, 29 November 1993, Paris.

[31] See François Heisbourg, 'The European–US Alliance: Valedictory Reflections on Continental Drift in the post-Cold War Era', *International Affairs*, vol. 68, no. 4, 1992, pp. 665–78, and the address of NATO's Secretary-General, Manfred Wörner, to the WEU Assembly, 29 November 1993, Paris.

[32] See *Atlantic News*, no. 2471, 11 November 1992, pp. 1 and 2.

[33] See Schmidt, *The Special Franco-German Security Relationship*, pp. 40–45.

[34] See Luisa Vierucci, *WEU: A Regional Partner of the United Nations?*, Chaillot Paper 12 (Paris: WEU Institute for Security Studies, December 1993).

[35] See Jennone Walker, 'Fact and Fiction about a European Security Identity and American Interests', The Atlantic Council of the United States, Occasional Paper, March 1992.

[36] See also Mortimer, *European Security after the Cold War*, Chapter IV.

[37] See, for example, Samuel Huntington, 'America's Changing Strategic Interests', *Survival*, vol. 33, no. 1, January–February 1991, pp. 3–17.

[38] See the speech by William Taft, IISS, London, February 1991.

[39] See Heisbourg, 'The European–US Alliance', p. 671, and Dieter Mahnke, *Parameters of European Security*, Chaillot Paper 10 (Paris: WEU Institute for Security Studies, September 1993), pp. 17, 32 and 33.

[40] See Peter Rudolf, 'The Strategic Debate in the USA – Implications for the American Role in Europe', *Aussenpolitik,* no. 2, 1993, pp. 111–19; Klaus-Dieter Schwarz, 'Die Entwicklung der amerikanischen Sicherheitspolitik mit Blick auf die künftigen Beziehungen zu Westeuropa', SWP-AP 2795 (Ebenhausen: Stiftung Wissenschaft und Politik, May 1993).

[41] See the speech by President Bill Clinton, Brussels, 9 January 1994, *Europe Documents*, no. 1868, 14 January 1994.

[42] See *Livre Blanc sur la Défense* (Paris: Ministère de la défense, 1994), pp. 52–57.

[43] See Peter Schmidt, 'French Security Ambitions', *Aussenpolitik*, vol. 44, no. 4, 1993, pp. 335–43.

[44] See Bernhard May, 'Der erfolgreiche GATT-Abschluss – ein Pyrrhussieg?' *Europa-Archiv,* no. 2, 1994, pp. 33–42.

[45] See Michael Brenner, 'Multilateralism and European Security', *Survival*, vol. 35, no. 2, Summer 1993, pp. 138–55, and Brenner, 'EC: Confidence Lost', *Foreign Policy*, no. 91, Summer 1993, pp. 24–43.

[46] See 'Decisions Taken at the Meeting of the North Atlantic Council on 9 August 1993', *NATO Press Release* (93) 53; see also the press statement of the Secretary-General following the special meeting of NAC in Brussels, 2 August 1993.

[47] See communiqué of the North Atlantic Council, 9 February 1994.

[48] See Uwe Nerlich, 'Neue Sicherheitsfunktionen der NATO', *Europa-Archiv*, no. 23, 1993, pp. 663–72.

[49] President Clinton, *Europe Documents*, no. 1868, 14 January 1994, p. 2.

[50] See Ian Davidson, 'Alive but Ailing: NATO is not the Solution to the Future Security Needs of Europe', *Financial Times*, 12 January 1994, p. 12.

[51] See *Le débat stratégique*, no. 12, January 1994, p. 1.

[52] See Trevor Taylor, 'West European Security and Defence Cooperation: Maastricht and Beyond', *International Affairs*, vol. 70, no. 1, 1994, pp. 1–16.

[53] See US Secretary of State Warren Christopher, 'Towards a NATO Summit', *NATO Review*, vol. 41, no. 4, August 1993, pp. 3–6.

[54] See Pierre Lellouche, 'France in Search of Security', *Foreign Affairs*, vol. 72, no. 2, spring 1993, pp. 121–31.

[55] See Roberto Zadra, *European Integration and Nuclear Deterrence after the Cold War*, Chaillot Paper 5 (Paris: WEU Institute for Security Studies, November 1992).

[56] See Delors, 'European Integration and Security', particularly p. 109.

[57] See Nanette Gantz and John Roper (eds), *Towards a New Transatlantic Partnership. US–European Relations in the post-Cold War Era* (Paris: WEU Institute for Security Studies, 1993), particularly pp. 167–84.

[58] See Uwe Nerlich, 'Deutsche Sicherheitspolitik: konzeptionelle Grundlagen für multilaterale Rahmenbedienungen', SWP-AP 2822 (Ebenhausen: Stiftung Wissenschaft und Politik, January 1994).

[59] See speech by Foreign Minister Kinkel at the Foreign Policy Congress of the Free Democratic Party in Bonn, 10 September 1993, reprinted in French in Bulletin no. 13 of the German Embassy, Paris.

Chapter III

[1] See John Mearsheimer, 'Back to the Future: Instability in Europe after the Cold War', *International Security*, vol. 15, no. 1, Summer 1990, pp. 5–56, and Josef Joffe, 'The New Europe: Yesterday's Ghosts', *Foreign Affairs*, vol. 72, no. 1, 1993, pp. 29–43.

[2] See Trevor C. Salmon, 'Testing Times for European Political Cooperation: the Gulf and Yugoslavia, 1990–1992', *International Affairs*, vol. 68, no. 2, 1992, pp. 233–53; Nicole Gnesotto and John Roper (eds), *Western Europe and the Gulf* (Paris: the Institute for Security Studies, WEU, 1992).

[3] For a general analysis of the complexity of the Yugoslav conflict, see Hans Stark, *Les Balkans. Le retour de la guerre en Europe* (Paris: IFRI-Dunod, 1993); John Zametica, *The Yugoslav Conflict*, Adelphi Paper 270 (London: Brassey's for the IISS, 1992); and James Gow, 'Deconstructing Yugoslavia', *Survival*, vol. 33, no. 4, July–August 1991, pp. 291–311.

[4] For France's Yugoslav policies, see Ronald Tiersky, 'France in the New Europe', *Foreign Affairs*, vol. 71, no. 2, Spring 1992, pp. 131–46.

[5] See Heinz-Jürgen Axt, 'Hat Genscher Jugoslawien entzweit? Mythen und Fakten zur Aussenpolitik des vereinten Deutschlands', *Europa-Archiv*, no. 12, 1993, pp. 351–60.

[6] For the guidelines as concluded by the Twelve on 16 December 1991, see *Agence Europe*, no. 5632, 18 December 1991, pp. 3 and 4.

[7] See Catherine Guicherd, 'L'heure de l'Europe, premières leçons du conflit yougoslave', *Cahier du CREST*, no. 10, March 1993; 'The Yugoslav Conflict – Chronology of Events from 30 May 1991 to 8 November 1993', *Information Document of the WEU Assembly*, Paris, 29 November 1993 (A/WEU/DEF(93)14).

[8] See the Goerens report, 'European Union and Developments in Central and Eastern Europe', *WEU Assembly*

Document, no. 1293, 27 November 1991; the De Hoop Scheffer report, 'Operational Arrangements for WEU – the Yugoslav Crisis', *WEU Assembly Document,* no. 1294, 27 November 1991; the Roseta report, 'Activities of the WEU Council', *WEU Assembly Document,* no. 1285, 6 November 1991.

[9] See Nicole Gnesotto, *Lessons of Yugoslavia* Chaillot Paper 14 (Paris: WEU Institute for Security Studies, March 1994); Sir Russell Johnston's report, 'Lessons Drawn from the Yugoslav Conflict', *WEU Assembly Document,* no. 1395, 9 November 1993.

[10] See Peter Schmidt, 'Die Sicherheitspolitik der EG-Staaten und die Vereinten Nationen. Konsequenzen für die Aussenpolitik Deutschlands', SWP-IP 2800 (Ebenhausen: Stiftung Wissenschaft und Politik, June 1993).

[11] See the Soell report, 'Political Relations between the United Nations and WEU and their Consequences for the development of WEU', *WEU Assembly Document,* no. 1389, 8 November 1993.

[12] See the Petersberg Declaration of 19 June 1992, Part I.

[13] The communiqué of the Forum of Consultation, 20 May 1993, stated only that 'Ministers agreed that, were any country to suffer from an aggressive action as a consequence of their support for UN mandated operations, this would be a matter of direct concern to the international community'.

[14] See Bassam Tibi, 'Die islamische Dimension des Balkan-Krieges', *Europa-Archiv,* no. 22, 1993, pp. 635–44.

[15] See Trevor Taylor, 'NATO and Central Europe: Problems and Opportunities in a new Relationship', Royal Institute of International Affairs (RIIA), Discussion Paper no. 39, 1992, and Andrzej Podraza, 'Western European Union and Central Europe. A New Relationship', RIIA, Discussion Paper no. 41, 1992.

[16] See the declaration issued by the enlarged WEU Council meeting, Petersberg, 19 June 1992, *Europe Documents,* no. 1787, 23 June 1992.

[17] See Ronald D. Asmus, Richard L. Kugler and Stephen Larrabee, 'Building a New NATO', *Foreign Affairs,* vol. 72, no. 4, September–October 1993, pp. 28–40; Volker Rühe, 'Shaping Euro-Atlantic Policies: a Grand Strategy for a New Era', *Survival,* vol. 35, no. 2, Summer 1993, pp. 129–37.

[18] See 'Partnership for Peace: Invitation', issued by the heads of state and government at the NAC meeting, Brussels, 10–11 January 1994, and the PFP framework document annexed to it.

[19] See Uwe Nerlich, 'Jenseits des Partnership for Peace Programms', SWP-AP 2821 (Ebenhausen: Stiftung Wissenschaft und Politik, January 1994).

[20] See the declaration of the WEU Council of Ministers, Luxembourg, 22 November 1993, Part I, para. 5; for the Franco-German proposal, see 'Déclaration commune des ministres des affaires étrangères d'Allemagne, de Pologne et de France', Warsaw, 12 November 1993, para. 4.2.

[21] For the French memorandum of 9 June 1993, see *Europe Documents,* no. 1846, 26 June 1993.

[22] See Jonathan Eyal, 'France's False Sense of Security', *The Independent,* 27 January 1994, p. 23.

[23] See Conclusions of the Presidency, European Council of Brussels, 10–11 December 1993, *Agence Europe,* no.

For Product Safety Concerns and Information please contact our EU
representative GPSR@taylorandfrancis.com
Taylor & Francis Verlag GmbH, Kaufingerstraße 24, 80331 München, Germany

www.ingramcontent.com/pod-product-compliance
Ingram Content Group UK Ltd.
Pitfield, Milton Keynes, MK11 3LW, UK
UKHW021437080625
459435UK00011B/283